Go Programming Essentials

Writing Efficient and Scalable Applications Learn Go for backend development, cloud computing, and microservices

THOMPSON CARTER

Table of Content

TABLE OF CONTENTS

Introduction

Welcome to *Go Programming Essentials: Writing Efficient and Scalable Applications*. This book is designed to take you on a comprehensive journey through the Go programming language, from the fundamentals to advanced techniques for building high-performance, scalable applications. Whether you're new to Go or have some experience with other programming languages, this book will provide you with the tools, strategies, and insights needed to harness Go's full potential.

Why Go?

Go, also known as **Golang**, is a statically typed, compiled programming language developed by Google. Its design emphasizes simplicity, efficiency, and concurrency, making it a go-to choice for building scalable and high-performance applications. Go is widely used in industries ranging from cloud infrastructure to web development, data science, and distributed systems. Its robust concurrency model, strong standard library, and excellent tooling make it a fantastic option for developing modern, complex software systems.

Over the years, Go has proven itself in the realm of backend services, cloud computing, and microservices architecture. This book aims to guide you through leveraging Go to its fullest, helping you build efficient applications that can scale easily and handle complex workloads.

Who Should Read This Book?

This book is written for developers who want to learn Go and take full advantage of its capabilities. It is suitable for:

- **Beginners**: If you're new to Go or programming in general, this book will help you grasp the basics and build a solid foundation. You'll gradually build up to more complex concepts such as concurrency and scalable system design.
- **Intermediate Developers**: If you're familiar with Go but want to deepen your understanding of its advanced features, this book will introduce you to performance optimization techniques, real-world architectures, and best practices.
- **Experienced Developers**: If you're an experienced developer working with systems programming or cloud-native development, you'll find in-depth coverage of concurrency, real-time applications, testing, CI/CD, and

21

scaling solutions to meet the demands of modern software development.

What You Will Learn

Throughout this book, you'll learn how to develop high-performance, scalable applications using Go, including:

- **Go Basics**: Master Go's syntax, variables, data types, and control structures. Learn how Go's simplicity makes it an ideal language for both new and experienced developers.
- **Concurrency**: Discover Go's powerful concurrency model, including goroutines and channels, which allow you to write applications that handle concurrent operations efficiently.
- **Go for Backend Development**: Learn how to build robust backend systems, including REST APIs, database integration, and authentication techniques.
- **Real-Time Applications**: Explore WebSockets and how to handle real-time data streaming, including building a real-time chat application.
- **Performance Optimization**: Dive into tools and techniques for benchmarking, profiling, and optimizing Go applications for speed and memory usage.
- **Testing and CI/CD**: Learn best practices for unit testing, integration testing, and setting up continuous integration

and continuous deployment pipelines to automate the testing and deployment process.

- **Cloud-Native Development**: Explore how Go is used for cloud-native applications, including containerization with Docker, deployment to Kubernetes, and service discovery with Consul.

Why This Book?

This book is designed to offer a hands-on, practical approach to learning Go. It is filled with **real-world examples** and **step-by-step tutorials** that demonstrate how to use Go in a wide range of applications, from web services and microservices to data processing and real-time systems. By the end of the book, you will not only have learned how to write Go code but also how to build and deploy full-scale, high-performance systems.

How This Book is Structured

The book is divided into **five main parts**:

1. **Foundations of Go Programming**: A deep dive into the syntax, data structures, and basic programming concepts in Go. This section covers the essentials, setting up a solid foundation for further learning.

2. **Go for Backend Development**: Focused on backend development with Go, including RESTful APIs, working with databases, security, and performance considerations.

3. **Cloud Computing and Microservices**: Learn how to scale Go applications with cloud-based technologies, including Docker, Kubernetes, and microservices architectures. This section introduces cloud-native practices, real-time applications, and deployment strategies.

4. **Advanced Go Programming**: Explore more complex topics like concurrency patterns, optimization techniques, and building highly scalable applications. You'll also learn how to integrate real-time data handling into your applications.

5. **Testing, CI/CD, and Deployment**: Learn how to implement automated testing, set up continuous integration pipelines, and deploy Go applications to production environments seamlessly.

Real-World Examples

Each chapter is filled with **hands-on projects**, **code snippets**, and **real-world scenarios** that demonstrate Go in action. Whether it's building a chat application, optimizing a backend service, or scaling a microservices-based platform, the examples help solidify your understanding of Go's capabilities and best practices.

Learning Through Practice

To complement the theoretical knowledge, the book encourages a **learning-by-doing** approach. Every major concept is followed by practical exercises, so you can apply what you've learned immediately. As you progress, you'll develop a series of small projects that culminate in full-fledged applications that can handle real-world problems.

Join the Go Community

Go has a vibrant, active community that's always growing. By learning Go, you are joining a community of developers who are shaping the future of software development. Throughout the book, you'll be directed to useful resources, such as documentation, forums, open-source libraries, and online communities, where you can seek help, share knowledge, and contribute to the Go ecosystem.

Conclusion

The **Go Programming Essentials** book is more than just a guide to learning Go; it's an invitation to enter the world of **high-performance software development**. Whether you're building a small web application or a complex distributed system, Go's simple syntax, powerful concurrency model, and fast execution make it an excellent choice for creating scalable and efficient applications. By the end of this book, you will be equipped with the knowledge and skills to tackle modern software challenges, build high-quality Go applications, and be prepared to continue your learning journey.

Welcome to the world of Go! Let's get started.

PART 1

FOUNDATIONS OF GO PROGRAMMING

CHAPTER 1

INTRODUCTION TO GO AND ITS ECOSYSTEM

1.1 Why Go? Performance, Concurrency, and Scalability

Go, also known as **Golang**, was developed by **Google** to address common challenges in software development: **performance bottlenecks, inefficient concurrency handling, and lack of scalability** in modern applications.

Here's why Go stands out:

1.1.1 Performance

- **Compiled Language:** Unlike Python and JavaScript, Go is a **compiled** language, meaning it translates code directly into machine code, making it significantly **faster** than interpreted languages.
- **Garbage Collection:** Go includes an optimized **garbage collector** that minimizes memory leaks and improves runtime performance.
- **Efficient Memory Management:** Unlike C and C++, Go abstracts away manual memory management while still providing speed close to those languages.

1.1.2 Concurrency

- **Goroutines vs. Threads:** Instead of using expensive system threads, Go introduces **goroutines**, which are lightweight and efficient, enabling true concurrency.
- **Channels for Communication:** Go provides **channels**, which allow goroutines to communicate without race conditions.

Example: Running multiple tasks concurrently in Go:

```go
go

package main

import (
    "fmt"
    "time"
)

func printMessage(msg string) {
    for i := 0; i < 5; i++ {
        fmt.Println(msg)
        time.Sleep(time.Millisecond * 500)
    }
}

func main() {
    go printMessage("Hello from Goroutine!")
```

```
    printMessage("Hello from Main function!")
}
```

This example runs `printMessage` concurrently without blocking execution.

1.1.3 Scalability

Go is built with **scalability** in mind:

- **Microservices Friendly:** Many companies (e.g., Uber, Netflix, Dropbox) use Go to build microservices due to its efficiency in handling large-scale distributed systems.
- **Cloud-Native Development:** Go is optimized for cloud environments, making it a popular choice for Kubernetes, Docker, and serverless applications.
- **Cross-Platform Support:** Write once, run anywhere— Go compiles to Windows, macOS, Linux, and ARM architectures.

1.2 Comparing Go with Python, Java, and C++

To understand Go's unique position, let's compare it with **Python, Java, and C++**:

Feature	Go	Python	Java	C++
Performance	Fast (compiled)	Slow (interpreted)	High (JVM-based)	Very fast (compiled)
Concurrency	Built-in Goroutines	Requires threading libraries	Uses heavy-weight threads	Uses OS threads
Memory Management	Garbage Collection	Garbage Collection	Garbage Collection	Manual Memory Management
Compilation	Compiled to binary	Interpreted	Compiled to bytecode (JVM)	Compiled to machine code
Ease of Use	Simple and clean syntax	Very easy to learn	Verbose syntax	Complex syntax
Microservices	Highly optimized	Not ideal for large-scale	Widely used in	Not ideal for microservices

Feature	Go	Python	Java	C++
		microservice s	enterprise s	

Key Takeaways:

- **Go vs. Python:** Python is great for scripting and AI, but Go is better for high-performance backend systems.
- **Go vs. Java:** Java is enterprise-friendly, but Go has a simpler concurrency model and faster execution.
- **Go vs. C++:** C++ provides fine-grained control over memory, but Go removes the complexity of manual memory management.

1.3 Real-World Applications of Go

Many major tech companies have adopted Go for its efficiency and scalability. Some notable use cases:

1. **Google (Cloud Services & Kubernetes)**
   - Kubernetes, the most popular container orchestration system, is **written in Go**.
   - Google's cloud services leverage Go for high-performance applications.

2. **Uber (Geolocation & Routing Systems)**

   o Uber migrated parts of its **real-time geolocation** services to Go, improving speed and reducing memory usage.

3. **Dropbox (High-Performance File Storage)**

   o Dropbox switched from Python to Go for its file synchronization backend, reducing CPU usage by **50%**.

4. **Netflix (Microservices Architecture)**

   o Go helps Netflix manage its **backend microservices**, handling millions of requests per second.

5. **Twitch (Streaming Services)**

   o Twitch uses Go to manage large-scale concurrent streaming services.

1.4 Setting Up the Go Development Environment

Before writing Go code, you need to install Go and set up your workspace.

1.4.1 Installing Go

1. **Download Go**

   o Go to the official Go website: https://go.dev/dl/

- o Download the installer for your OS (Windows, macOS, Linux).

2. **Verify Installation**

   - o Open the terminal and type:

```sh
```

```
go version
```

   - o You should see the installed Go version.

3. **Setting Up GOPATH**

   - o By default, Go uses `$HOME/go` as its workspace.
   - o Check your Go workspace:

```sh
```

```
go env GOPATH
```

   - o If needed, set a custom path by adding this to your shell configuration file (`.bashrc`, `.zshrc`, etc.):

```sh
```

```
export GOPATH=$HOME/go
export PATH=$GOPATH/bin:$PATH
```

1.4.2 Writing Your First Go Program

Let's create a simple **Hello, World!** program in Go.

1. **Create a new Go file (`hello.go`):**

```go
go

package main

import "fmt"

func main() {
    fmt.Println("Hello, Go!")
}
```

2. **Run the program:**

```sh
sh

go run hello.go
```

   o   Output:

```
Hello, Go!
```

3. **Compiling a Go Program**
   o   To compile Go into an executable:

```sh
sh

go build hello.go
```

- o This generates a binary file (`hello` or `hello.exe`).
- o Run it:

```sh

./hello    # On Linux/macOS
hello.exe # On Windows
```

1.4.3 Setting Up a Go Project

Go uses **modules** to manage dependencies.

1. **Initialize a Go module**:

```sh

go mod init myproject
```

2. **Create a Go file (main.go)**:

```go

package main

import "fmt"

func main() {
```

```
    fmt.Println("Go      Project      Setup
Complete!")
}
```

3. **Run the project**:

```sh
sh
```

```
go run main.go
```

1.5 Summary

- **Go is built for performance, concurrency, and scalability**, making it ideal for backend systems, cloud computing, and microservices.
- **Compared to Python, Java, and C++**, Go strikes a balance between speed, simplicity, and efficiency.
- **Real-world applications** include major companies like **Google, Uber, Dropbox, and Netflix**.
- **Setting up Go** is straightforward, with built-in support for dependency management and compilation.

Next Chapter: Basic Syntax and Data Types

In the next chapter, we'll cover Go's **variables, data types, structs, arrays, slices, and maps**, along with examples to solidify your understanding.

CHAPTER 2

BASIC SYNTAX AND DATA TYPES

Go has a clean and straightforward syntax that makes it easy to read and maintain. In this chapter, we will cover the fundamental building blocks of Go, including **variables, constants, data types, structs, arrays, slices, maps, loops, and conditionals**.

2.1 Variables, Constants, and Data Types

2.1.1 Declaring Variables in Go

In Go, you can declare variables using the `var` keyword or the shorthand `:=` notation.

Using `var` (Explicit Type Declaration)

go

```
var name string = "Go Programming"
var age int = 25
var price float64 = 99.99
var isAvailable bool = true
```

Using := (Type Inference)

Go allows shorthand variable declaration, where the type is inferred from the value.

go

```
name := "Go Programming"
age := 25
price := 99.99
isAvailable := true
```

Multiple Variable Declaration

go

```
var x, y, z int = 10, 20, 30
a, b, c := "Hello", 3.14, false
```

2.1.2 Constants in Go

Constants are declared using the `const` keyword and cannot be modified after declaration.

go

```
const Pi float64 = 3.14159
const AppName = "MyGoApp"
```

- Constants **must** be assigned a value at the time of declaration.

- You cannot use : = shorthand for constants.

2.1.3 Data Types in Go

Go is statically typed, meaning variables must have a specific type.

Type	Description	Example
int	Integer (whole numbers)	`var x int = 42`
float64	Floating-point numbers	`var price float64 = 99.99`
string	Sequence of characters	`var name string = "Go"`
bool	Boolean (true or false)	`var isActive bool = true`
byte	Alias for uint8	`var b byte = 255`
rune	Alias for int32 (Unicode)	`var r rune = 'A'`

2.2 Structs, Arrays, Slices, and Maps

2.2.1 Structs in Go

A **struct** is a custom data type that groups related fields together.

```go

package main

import "fmt"

type Person struct {
    Name  string
    Age   int
    Email string
}

func main() {
    person1 := Person{Name: "Alice", Age: 30, Email: "alice@example.com"}
    fmt.Println(person1.Name, "is", person1.Age, "years old.")
}
```

Use Case: Structs are useful when working with **objects** like user profiles, orders, or products.

2.2.2 Arrays in Go

An **array** is a fixed-size collection of elements of the same type.

go

```
var numbers [5]int // Array of size 5
numbers[0] = 10
numbers[1] = 20
numbers[2] = 30

fmt.Println(numbers) // Output: [10 20 30 0 0]
```

Limitation: Arrays have a **fixed length**, making them less flexible.

2.2.3 Slices in Go

A **slice** is a dynamic-sized array that is more commonly used than arrays.

go

```
nums  :=  []int{1,  2,  3,  4,  5}    // Slice
initialization
nums = append(nums, 6)          // Add an element

fmt.Println(nums) // Output: [1 2 3 4 5 6]
```

Slicing an Array/Slice

go

```
subSlice := nums[1:4] // Extracts elements from
index 1 to 3
fmt.Println(subSlice) // Output: [2 3 4]
```

Why Slices? Unlike arrays, slices can grow dynamically.

2.2.4 Maps in Go

A **map** is a key-value data structure.

go

```
user := map[string]string{
    "name":  "John Doe",
    "email": "john@example.com",
}

fmt.Println(user["name"]) // Output: John Doe

// Adding a new key-value pair
user["age"] = "30"

// Deleting a key
```

```
delete(user, "email")
```

Use Case: Maps are great for **storing configurations, JSON data, and caching.**

2.3 Control Structures: Loops and Conditionals

2.3.1 If-Else Statements

```go
go

package main

import "fmt"

func main() {
    age := 18

    if age >= 18 {
        fmt.Println("You are an adult.")
    } else {
        fmt.Println("You are a minor.")
    }
}
```

Go does not have a ternary operator (? :), so you must use if-else.

45

2.3.2 Switch Statements

Go's `switch` is **faster** than multiple `if-else` statements.

```go
package main

import "fmt"

func main() {
    day := "Monday"

    switch day {
    case "Monday":
        fmt.Println("Start of the workweek!")
    case "Friday":
        fmt.Println("Almost the weekend!")
    default:
        fmt.Println("It's just another day.")
    }
}
```

Use Case: Switch is ideal when checking **multiple conditions**.

2.3.3 Loops in Go

Go only has **one** looping construct: for.

Basic For Loop

go

```go
for i := 0; i < 5; i++ {
    fmt.Println("Iteration:", i)
}
```

For-Range Loop (Used with Slices and Maps)

go

```go
numbers := []int{10, 20, 30}

for index, value := range numbers {
    fmt.Println("Index:", index, "Value:", value)
}
```

While-like Loop (For without condition)

go

```go
i := 0
for i < 5 {
    fmt.Println(i)
    i++
}
```

Use Case: Loops are used for **iteration, automation, and data processing.**

2.4 Summary

- **Variables & Constants:** `var` for explicit type declaration, `:=` for inferred type.
- **Data Types:** `int`, `float64`, `string`, `bool`, `struct`, `map`, `slice`.
- **Structs:** Used for defining custom data types.
- **Arrays vs. Slices:** Arrays are **fixed-size**, slices are **dynamic**.
- **Maps:** Key-value pairs, useful for **lookup tables**.
- **Control Structures:** `if-else`, `switch`, and `for` loops.

Next Chapter: Functions and Error Handling

In the next chapter, we'll explore:

- **How to write functions in Go.**
- **Error handling best practices.**
- **Returning multiple values from functions.**

Would you like to include **hands-on exercises** at the end of each chapter to reinforce learning?

CHAPTER 3

FUNCTIONS AND ERROR HANDLING IN GO

Functions are the building blocks of any Go program, helping to structure code for **reusability, modularity, and maintainability**. Error handling in Go is explicit and robust, providing control over program execution.

In this chapter, we will cover:

- Writing functions in Go.
- Multiple return values.
- Handling errors with the `error` type.
- Using `panic` and `recover` for error recovery.

3.1 Writing Functions in Go

A **function** in Go is a block of reusable code that performs a specific task.

3.1.1 Basic Function Declaration

Syntax:

```go
func functionName(parameters) returnType {
    // Function body
    return value
}
```

Example:

```go
package main

import "fmt"

func greet(name string) string {
    return "Hello, " + name + "!"
}

func main() {
    message := greet("Alice")
    fmt.Println(message)
}
```

Explanation:

- The function greet takes a **string** parameter.

- It returns a **string** message.
- The `main` function calls `greet`, and prints the returned message.

3.1.2 Functions with Multiple Parameters

go

```go
func add(a int, b int) int {
    return a + b
}

func main() {
    sum := add(10, 20)
    fmt.Println("Sum:", sum)
}
```

Shortcut: If multiple parameters have the same type, you can declare them concisely:

go

```go
func add(a, b int) int {
    return a + b
}
```

3.1.3 Functions Without Return Values

Functions can **perform an action without returning anything**:

go

```go
func printMessage(msg string) {
    fmt.Println("Message:", msg)
}

func main() {
    printMessage("Go is awesome!")
}
```

3.1.4 Variadic Functions (Functions with Unlimited Arguments)

Go supports **variadic functions**, which accept an indefinite number of arguments.

go

```go
func sum(numbers ...int) int {
    total := 0
    for _, num := range numbers {
        total += num
```

```
    }
    return total
}

func main() {
    fmt.Println("Total:", sum(1, 2, 3, 4, 5))
}
```

Explanation:

- ...int allows the function to accept **multiple integers**.
- The range loop iterates over all arguments.

3.2 Multiple Return Values

Go allows functions to return **multiple values**.

3.2.1 Returning Multiple Values

go

```
func divide(a, b float64) (float64, string) {
    if b == 0 {
        return 0, "Error: Division by zero"
    }
    return a / b, ""
}
```

```go
func main() {
    result, err := divide(10, 2)
    if err != "" {
        fmt.Println(err)
    } else {
        fmt.Println("Result:", result)
    }
}
```

Explanation:

- If division by zero occurs, the function returns an **error message**.
- Otherwise, it returns the division result.

3.2.2 Named Return Values

You can name return values **inside the function signature**:

go

```go
func fullName(first, last string) (name string)
{
    name = first + " " + last
    return
}
```

```go
func main() {
    fmt.Println(fullName("John", "Doe"))
}
```

Benefit: You don't need to explicitly specify `return` name;—just `return` is enough.

3.3 Handling Errors with the `error` Type

Unlike many languages, Go **does not use exceptions** for error handling. Instead, functions return an `error` type.

3.3.1 Using the `error` Type

```go
go

import "errors"

func divide(a, b float64) (float64, error) {
    if b == 0 {
        return 0, errors.New("cannot divide by zero")
    }
    return a / b, nil
}

func main() {
```

```go
    result, err := divide(10, 0)
    if err != nil {
        fmt.Println("Error:", err)
    } else {
        fmt.Println("Result:", result)
    }
}
```

Explanation:

- `errors.New("message")` creates an **error object**.
- The function returns `(value, error)`, where `nil` means **no error**.

3.3.2 Custom Error Types

Go allows **custom error handling** with `fmt.Errorf`:

go

```go
import "fmt"

func divide(a, b float64) (float64, error) {
    if b == 0 {
        return 0, fmt.Errorf("cannot divide %f by zero", a)
    }
```

```
    return a / b, nil
}
```

3.4 Panic and Recover in Go

While Go **avoids exceptions**, it provides `panic` and `recover` for **handling unexpected errors**.

3.4.1 Using `panic` to Forcefully Stop Execution

`panic` **stops the program** immediately.

```go
package main

import "fmt"

func checkAge(age int) {
    if age < 18 {
        panic("Age must be 18 or older!")
    }
    fmt.Println("Access granted")
}

func main() {
    checkAge(15) // This will trigger panic
}
```

Use Case: `panic` is used when the program cannot proceed (e.g., missing config files, failed database connection).

3.4.2 Recovering from a Panic

`recover` **prevents a crash** and allows cleanup before exiting.

```go
package main

import "fmt"

func safeDivide(a, b int) {
    defer func() {
        if r := recover(); r != nil {
            fmt.Println("Recovered from panic:",
r)
        }
    }()

    if b == 0 {
        panic("Division by zero")
    }

    fmt.Println("Result:", a/b)
```

```
}

func main() {
    safeDivide(10, 0)
    fmt.Println("Program      continues       after
handling panic")
}
```

Explanation:

- `defer func()` waits for a **panic**.
- `recover()` **captures** the panic message and prevents the crash.

3.5 Summary

Concept	Description
Functions	Defined with `func`, can take multiple parameters and return values.
Multiple Return Values	Functions can return multiple values, including `error`.
Error Handling	Go does **not** use exceptions, instead, functions return an `error` object.
panic	Stops program execution immediately.

Concept	Description
recover	Captures panic to prevent crashes.

Next Chapter: Working with Pointers and Memory Management

In the next chapter, we'll explore:

- **Pointers in Go**
- **Passing by value vs. reference**
- **Memory management and garbage collection**

CHAPTER 4

WORKING WITH POINTERS AND MEMORY MANAGEMENT IN GO

Memory management is crucial for writing efficient and scalable applications. Go simplifies memory handling with **garbage collection**, but understanding **pointers** and how **data is passed in functions** helps in writing optimized code.

4.1 Understanding Pointers in Go

A **pointer** is a variable that stores the memory address of another variable. Instead of holding a value, it holds the **reference** to the value.

4.1.1 Declaring and Using Pointers

In Go, a pointer is declared using the * operator.

```go
go
```

```
package main
```

```
import "fmt"

func main() {
    var x int = 10
    var p *int = &x   // Pointer to x

    fmt.Println("Value of x:", x)        // 10
    fmt.Println("Memory address of x:", &x)
    fmt.Println("Pointer p points to:", p)
    fmt.Println("Value at pointer p:", *p)   //
Dereferencing
}
```

Explanation

- &x gives the **memory address** of x (pointer reference).
- p stores the **address** of x.
- *p (**dereferencing**) retrieves the **value stored at that address**.

4.1.2 Changing Values Using Pointers

Pointers allow functions to modify variables directly.

go

```
package main
```

63

```go
import "fmt"

func modifyValue(p *int) {
    *p = 20 // Modifies the original variable
}

func main() {
    x := 10
    fmt.Println("Before:", x)

    modifyValue(&x) // Pass memory address of x
    fmt.Println("After:", x)
}
```

Use Case: Pointers help when passing large data structures efficiently.

4.2 Passing by Value vs. Passing by Reference

In Go, function arguments are **passed by value** by default, meaning changes inside the function **don't affect** the original variable.

4.2.1 Passing by Value

go

```go
func doubleValue(num int) {
    num = num * 2
}

func main() {
    x := 10
    doubleValue(x)
    fmt.Println("Value of x:", x) // x remains 10
}
```

Why? Because num is a of x.

4.2.2 Passing by Reference (Using Pointers)

Using pointers allows modifying the original variable.

```go
go
```

```go
func doubleValue(num *int) {
    *num = *num * 2
}

func main() {
    x := 10
    doubleValue(&x) // Pass memory address
```

```
    fmt.Println("Value   of   x:",   x)  //  x   is
modified to 20
}
```

Best Practice: Use **passing by reference** when working with **large data structures** to avoid unnecessary copies.

4.3 Memory Management in Go (Garbage Collection)

Unlike languages like C/C++, Go **automatically** manages memory using **garbage collection (GC)**.

4.3.1 How Go's Garbage Collector Works

- **Automatic Cleanup:** Unused memory is freed without manual intervention.
- **Tracing Algorithm:** The garbage collector identifies and removes objects **no longer reachable**.
- **Concurrency-Friendly:** GC runs in the background, ensuring minimal impact on performance.

4.3.2 Memory Allocation in Go

Go provides two primary ways to allocate memory:

1. **new Function** (Allocates memory, returns a pointer)
2. **make Function** (Used for slices, maps, and channels)

Using new (Allocating Memory)

go

```
package main

import "fmt"

func main() {
    p := new(int) // Allocates memory for an int
    fmt.Println("Value at pointer p:", *p) //
Default is 0

    *p = 42
    fmt.Println("Updated value:", *p)
}
```

Why use new?

- Allocates memory **on the heap**.
- Returns a **pointer** to the allocated memory.

Using make (For Slices, Maps, and Channels)

The make function is used for **dynamic structures**.

```go
s := make([]int, 5)   // Creates a slice of size 5
m := make(map[string]int)   // Creates a map
c := make(chan int)   // Creates a channel
```

Key Difference Between new and make:

- new **only allocates memory** and returns a pointer.
- make **initializes** slices, maps, and channels.

4.3.3 Avoiding Memory Leaks

Even though Go has GC, improper memory usage can lead to leaks.

✅ **Best Practices to Avoid Memory Leaks**

- **Close unused channels**

    ```go
    ch := make(chan int)
    close(ch)
    ```

- **Remove unused map keys**

```
go
```

```
delete(myMap, "key")
```

- **Limit use of goroutines**

```
go
```

```
go func() {
    for data := range myChannel {
        fmt.Println(data)
    }
}()
```

4.4 Summary

Concept	Description
Pointers	Store memory addresses of variables.
Dereferencing (*)	Retrieves value from a pointer.
Passing by Value	Function gets a of the variable.
Passing by Reference	Function gets a pointer, modifying the original variable.
Garbage Collection (GC)	Go automatically reclaims unused memory.

Concept	Description
new vs. make	`new` allocates memory, `make` initializes slices, maps, and channels.

Next Chapter: Structs, Interfaces, and Methods

In the next chapter, we'll explore:

- **Defining and using structs**
- **Implementing interfaces in Go**
- **Attaching methods to structs**

CHAPTER 5

STRUCTS, INTERFACES, AND METHODS IN GO

Structs and interfaces are **fundamental** to Go's object-oriented programming (OOP) model. Since Go **does not support classes**, it uses **structs** to define data types and **interfaces** to define behavior. In this chapter, we will explore:

- **Defining structs and methods.**
- **Implementing interfaces in Go.**
- **Building a simple user authentication system.**

5.1 Defining Structs and Methods

A **struct** is a collection of fields that represents an object with **related attributes**.

5.1.1 Declaring and Using Structs

go

```go
package main

import "fmt"

// Defining a struct
type User struct {
    Name  string
    Email string
    Age   int
}

func main() {
    // Initializing a struct
    user1 := User{"Alice", "alice@example.com",
30}
    fmt.Println("User:", user1)

    // Accessing struct fields
    fmt.Println("Name:", user1.Name)
    fmt.Println("Email:", user1.Email)
}
```

Explanation:

- User is a **struct type** with Name, Email, and Age fields.
- We **initialize** the struct using { }.
- Fields are accessed using **dot notation** (user1.Name).

5.1.2 Creating Structs with Named Fields

Instead of assigning values by order, **explicitly naming fields** improves readability.

go

```
user2 := User{
    Name:  "Bob",
    Email: "bob@example.com",
    Age:   25,
}
```

5.1.3 Pointer to a Struct

Structs can be used with **pointers** to allow modifications.

go

```
func updateEmail(u *User, newEmail string) {
    u.Email = newEmail
}

func main() {
    user              :=              User{"Charlie",
"charlie@example.com", 40}
    updateEmail(&user, "newemail@example.com")
    fmt.Println("Updated Email:", user.Email)
```

73

```
}
```

Why use pointers? Without pointers, a   of the struct is passed, and changes won't affect the original struct.

5.2 Implementing Methods in Go

Unlike traditional OOP languages, Go **attaches methods to structs** rather than using classes.

5.2.1 Defining Methods on Structs

```go
package main

import "fmt"

type User struct {
    Name   string
    Email string
}

// Method attached to User struct
func (u User) display() {
    fmt.Println("User:",    u.Name,    "Email:",
u.Email)
```

```
}

func main() {
    user := User{"Alice", "alice@example.com"}
    user.display() // Calling the method
}
```

Key Concept: The method `display()` has a **receiver** (u User), meaning it belongs to User.

5.2.2 Methods with Pointers (Modifying Struct Fields)

To modify a struct inside a method, use a **pointer receiver**.

go

```
func (u *User) changeEmail(newEmail string) {
    u.Email = newEmail
}

func main() {
    user := User{"Bob", "bob@example.com"}
    user.changeEmail("bob@newmail.com")
    fmt.Println("Updated Email:", user.Email)
}
```

Why pointer receiver? Without *User, the method operates on a of the struct, and changes won't persist.

5.3 Implementing Interfaces in Go

An **interface** is a **collection of method signatures**. Any struct that implements these methods **satisfies** the interface.

5.3.1 Defining and Using Interfaces

go

```
package main

import "fmt"

// Defining an interface
type Notifier interface {
    SendNotification()
}

// Struct implementing the interface
type EmailNotifier struct {
    Email string
}

// Implementing the interface method
```

```go
func (e EmailNotifier) SendNotification() {
    fmt.Println("Sending Email to:", e.Email)
}

func main() {
    email := EmailNotifier{"user@example.com"}
    email.SendNotification()  // Works because
EmailNotifier implements Notifier
}
```

Key Concept: Any struct that has a `SendNotification()` method **automatically** implements `Notifier`, without needing explicit declaration.

5.3.2 Using Interfaces in Functions

Functions can accept **any type** that implements an interface.

go

```go
func sendAlert(n Notifier) {
    n.SendNotification()
}

func main() {
    email := EmailNotifier{"alice@example.com"}
```

```go
    sendAlert(email)    //    Works    because
EmailNotifier satisfies Notifier
}
```

Why Interfaces? Interfaces allow writing **flexible** code where multiple types can share behavior.

5.3.3 Multiple Structs Implementing the Same Interface

go

```go
type SMSNotifier struct {
    PhoneNumber string
}

func (s SMSNotifier) SendNotification() {
    fmt.Println("Sending        SMS        to:",
s.PhoneNumber)
}

func main() {
    email := EmailNotifier{"bob@example.com"}
    sms := SMSNotifier{"123-456-7890"}

    sendAlert(email)
```

```
sendAlert(sms) // Works because both structs
implement Notifier
}
```

Advantage: Different structs (EmailNotifier, SMSNotifier) can be used interchangeably with `sendAlert()`.

5.4 Real-World Example: Building a Simple User Authentication System

We will build a **basic authentication system** using structs, methods, and interfaces.

5.4.1 Defining the User Struct

```go
go
```

```go
type User struct {
    Username string
    Password string
}
```

5.4.2 Adding an Authentication Method

```go
go
```

```go
func (u User) Authenticate(password string) bool
{
    return u.Password == password
}
```

5.4.3 Implementing Authentication

```go
go

package main

import "fmt"

// Struct to store user data
type User struct {
    Username string
    Password string
}

// Method to authenticate user
func (u User) Authenticate(password string) bool
{
    return u.Password == password
}

func main() {
    user := User{"alice", "secure123"}
```

```
var passwordInput string
fmt.Print("Enter password: ")
fmt.Scan(&passwordInput)

if user.Authenticate(passwordInput) {
    fmt.Println("Login successful!")
} else {
    fmt.Println("Incorrect password.")
}
}
```

How It Works:

- The **User struct** stores a username and password.
- `Authenticate()` method checks if the entered password matches the stored password.
- The program **prompts the user** for input and validates it.

5.5 Summary

Concept	Description
Structs	Define objects with multiple fields.
Methods	Functions attached to a struct.

Concept	Description
Pointer Receivers	Allow modifying struct fields inside methods.
Interfaces	Define behavior that multiple structs can implement.
Real-World Example	Implemented a basic user authentication system.

Next Chapter: Building REST APIs with Go

In the next chapter, we will:

- **Set up a basic REST API in Go.**
- **Use the net/http package to handle requests.**
- **Work with JSON for request and response handling.**

PART 2

GO FOR BACKEND
DEVELOPMENT

CHAPTER 6

BUILDING REST APIS WITH GO

In this chapter, we'll cover how to **set up a REST API** in Go, use the **net/http package** to handle HTTP requests, and work with **JSON data** using the **encoding/json package**. By the end of this chapter, you'll be able to build a basic RESTful API in Go.

6.1 Setting Up a Basic REST API

A **REST API** allows communication between a client (frontend or another service) and a backend server using **HTTP requests** (GET, POST, PUT, DELETE). Go's built-in **net/http package** makes it easy to create APIs without external frameworks.

6.1.1 Installing Go and Setting Up a Project

1. **Ensure Go is installed**

    sh

```
go version
```

If Go is not installed, download it from https://go.dev/dl/.

2. **Create a new project folder**

```sh
```

```
mkdir go-rest-api && cd go-rest-api
```

3. **Initialize a Go module**

```sh
```

```
go mod init go-rest-api
```

4. **Create a main.go file**

```sh
```

```
touch main.go
```

6.2 Using the net/http Package

The **net/http package** is Go's standard library for building web servers.

6.2.1 Creating a Simple HTTP Server

```go
package main

import (
    "fmt"
    "net/http"
)

func homeHandler(w http.ResponseWriter, r *http.Request) {
    fmt.Fprintf(w, "Welcome to the Go REST API!")
}

func main() {
    http.HandleFunc("/", homeHandler) // Route for homepage
    fmt.Println("Server running on port 8080...")
    http.ListenAndServe(":8080", nil) // Start server on port 8080
}
```

Explanation

- `http.HandleFunc("/", homeHandler)`: Registers a route that triggers `homeHandler`.

- `homeHandler()`: Handles incoming HTTP requests and sends a response.
- `http.ListenAndServe(":8080", nil)`: Starts the server on **port 8080**.

Run the server

```sh
sh
```

```
go run main.go
```

Visit `http://localhost:8080/` in your browser, and you'll see **"Welcome to the Go REST API!"**.

6.3 Handling JSON Data with `encoding/json`

APIs commonly send and receive data in **JSON format**. Go's `encoding/json` package helps in encoding and decoding JSON.

6.3.1 Creating a Simple API That Returns JSON

```go
go
```

```
package main
```

```go
import (
    "encoding/json"
    "net/http"
)

type Response struct {
    Message string `json:"message"`
}

func    jsonHandler(w    http.ResponseWriter,    r
*http.Request) {
    response := Response{Message: "Hello, this is
a JSON response!"}
    w.Header().Set("Content-Type",
"application/json")
    json.NewEncoder(w).Encode(response)
}

func main() {
    http.HandleFunc("/json", jsonHandler)
    http.ListenAndServe(":8080", nil)
}
```

Explanation

- The `Response` struct defines a JSON response with the
  `json:"message"` tag.
- `json.NewEncoder(w).Encode(response)` converts
  the struct into a JSON response.

- The `Content-Type: application/json` header ensures the client recognizes it as JSON.

Test it

Run   the   server   and   visit:

☞   `http://localhost:8080/json`

Response:

```
json
```

```
{"message":"Hello, this is a JSON response!"}
```

6.4 Building a CRUD REST API

Let's build a **CRUD (Create, Read, Update, Delete) API** for managing a list of books.

6.4.1 Define the Book Struct

```go
type Book struct {
    ID     int    `json:"id"`
    Title  string `json:"title"`
    Author string `json:"author"`
}
```

6.4.2 Create Sample Data

go

```go
var books = []Book{
    {ID: 1, Title: "The Go Programming Language",
Author: "Alan A. A. Donovan"},
    {ID: 2, Title: "Learning Go", Author: "Jon
Bodner"},
}
```

6.4.3 Implement API Endpoints

6.4.3.1 GET - Fetch All Books

go

```go
func    getBooks(w    http.ResponseWriter,    r
*http.Request) {
    w.Header().Set("Content-Type",
"application/json")
    json.NewEncoder(w).Encode(books)
}
```

Test with:

sh

```sh
curl -X GET http://localhost:8080/books
```

6.4.3.2 POST - Add a New Book

go

```go
func    createBook(w    http.ResponseWriter,    r
*http.Request) {
    var newBook Book
    json.NewDecoder(r.Body).Decode(&newBook)
    newBook.ID = len(books) + 1 // Assign a new
ID
    books = append(books, newBook)
    json.NewEncoder(w).Encode(newBook)
}
```

Test with:

sh

```sh
curl   -X   POST   http://localhost:8080/books   -H
"Content-Type:        application/json"        -d
'{"title":"Go    in    Action","author":"William
Kennedy"}'
```

6.4.3.3 PUT - Update a Book

go

```go
func    updateBook(w    http.ResponseWriter,    r
*http.Request) {
```

91

```go
    var updatedBook Book

json.NewDecoder(r.Body).Decode(&updatedBook)

    for index, book := range books {
        if book.ID == updatedBook.ID {
            books[index] = updatedBook

json.NewEncoder(w).Encode(updatedBook)
            return
        }
    }
    http.Error(w,      "Book     not      found",
http.StatusNotFound)
}
```

Test with:

sh

```sh
curl  -X  PUT  http://localhost:8080/books  -H
"Content-Type:      application/json"      -d
'{"id":1,"title":"Updated
Title","author":"Updated Author"}'
```

6.4.3.4 DELETE - Remove a Book

go

92

```go
func    deleteBook(w    http.ResponseWriter,    r
*http.Request) {
    var bookToDelete Book

json.NewDecoder(r.Body).Decode(&bookToDelete)

    for index, book := range books {
        if book.ID == bookToDelete.ID {
            books    =    append(books[:index],
books[index+1:]...)

json.NewEncoder(w).Encode(map[string]string{"me
ssage": "Book deleted"})
            return
        }
    }
    http.Error(w,    "Book    not    found",
http.StatusNotFound)
}
```

Test with:

sh

```sh
curl  -X  DELETE  http://localhost:8080/books  -H
"Content-Type: application/json" -d '{"id":1}'
```

6.4.4 Wiring Everything Together in `main.go`

```go
go

package main

import (
    "encoding/json"
    "fmt"
    "net/http"
)

type Book struct {
    ID     int    `json:"id"`
    Title  string `json:"title"`
    Author string `json:"author"`
}

var books = []Book{
    {ID: 1, Title: "The Go Programming Language",
Author: "Alan A. A. Donovan"},
    {ID: 2, Title: "Learning Go", Author: "Jon
Bodner"},
}

func getBooks(w http.ResponseWriter, r
*http.Request) {
    w.Header().Set("Content-Type",
"application/json")
    json.NewEncoder(w).Encode(books)
}
```

```go
func    createBook(w    http.ResponseWriter,    r
*http.Request) {
    var newBook Book
    json.NewDecoder(r.Body).Decode(&newBook)
    newBook.ID = len(books) + 1
    books = append(books, newBook)
    json.NewEncoder(w).Encode(newBook)
}

func main() {
    http.HandleFunc("/books", getBooks)
    http.HandleFunc("/books/add", createBook)

    fmt.Println("Server    running    on    port
8080...")
    http.ListenAndServe(":8080", nil)
}
```

6.5 Summary

Concept	Description
net/http package	Used to build REST APIs.
Handling JSON	encoding/json to parse and encode JSON.

Concept	Description
CRUD Operations	Implemented `GET`, `POST`, `PUT`, `DELETE` endpoints.

Next Chapter: Database Integration with Go

In the next chapter, we'll cover:

- **Connecting Go to PostgreSQL/MySQL.**
- **Performing CRUD operations with a database.**
- **Using ORM libraries like GORM.**

CHAPTER 7

DATABASE INTEGRATION WITH GO

Integrating a database into a Go application is essential for building scalable and persistent applications. In this chapter, we will explore:

- **Connecting Go to PostgreSQL and MySQL**
- **Performing CRUD operations using Go**
- **Using ORM libraries like GORM for simplified database handling**

7.1 Connecting Go to PostgreSQL and MySQL

Go provides native support for database interaction via the `database/sql` package, along with drivers for specific databases like **PostgreSQL** and **MySQL**.

7.1.1 Installing Required Packages

First, install the necessary database drivers.

For PostgreSQL

sh

```
go get github.com/lib/pq
```

For MySQL

sh

```
go get github.com/go-sql-driver/mysql
```

7.1.2 Connecting to PostgreSQL

go

```go
package main

import (
    "database/sql"
    "fmt"
    _ "github.com/lib/pq"
)

const (
    host     = "localhost"
    port     = 5432
    user     = "postgres"
    password = "yourpassword"
```

98

```
    dbname   = "testdb"
)


func main() {
    connStr  :=   fmt.Sprintf("host=%s   port=%d
user=%s password=%s dbname=%s sslmode=disable",
        host, port, user, password, dbname)

    db, err := sql.Open("postgres", connStr)
    if err != nil {
        panic(err)
    }
    defer db.Close()

    err = db.Ping()
    if err != nil {
        panic(err)
    }

    fmt.Println("Connected      to      PostgreSQL
successfully!")
}
```

7.1.3 Connecting to MySQL

go

```
package main
```

```go
import (
    "database/sql"
    "fmt"
    _ "github.com/go-sql-driver/mysql"
)

const (
    dsn                                          =
"root:yourpassword@tcp(127.0.0.1:3306)/testdb"
)

func main() {
    db, err := sql.Open("mysql", dsn)
    if err != nil {
        panic(err)
    }
    defer db.Close()

    err = db.Ping()
    if err != nil {
        panic(err)
    }

    fmt.Println("Connected       to       MySQL
successfully!")
}
```

Explanation:

- `sql.Open("driver-name", "connection-string")`: Opens a connection to the database.
- `db.Ping()`: Tests if the database connection is working.

7.2 CRUD Operations Using Go

Now, let's perform **Create, Read, Update, and Delete (CRUD)** operations in PostgreSQL/MySQL.

7.2.1 Creating a Table

For **PostgreSQL**, run the following SQL:

```sql
sql
```

```sql
CREATE TABLE users (
    id SERIAL PRIMARY KEY,
    name VARCHAR(100),
    email VARCHAR(100) UNIQUE
);
```

For **MySQL**, run:

```sql
sql
```

```sql
CREATE TABLE users (
    id INT AUTO_INCREMENT PRIMARY KEY,
```

```
name VARCHAR(100),
email VARCHAR(100) UNIQUE
);
```

7.2.2 Insert Data (CREATE)

go

```go
func createUser(db *sql.DB, name, email string)
{
    query := "INSERT INTO users (name, email)
VALUES ($1, $2)" // PostgreSQL
    _, err := db.Exec(query, name, email)
    if err != nil {
        panic(err)
    }
    fmt.Println("User added successfully!")
}
```

For **MySQL**, use ? instead of $1, $2:

go

```go
query := "INSERT INTO users (name, email) VALUES
(?, ?)"
```

7.2.3 Fetch Data (READ)

go

```go
func getUsers(db *sql.DB) {
    rows, err := db.Query("SELECT id, name, email FROM users")
    if err != nil {
        panic(err)
    }
    defer rows.Close()

    for rows.Next() {
        var id int
        var name, email string
        rows.Scan(&id, &name, &email)
        fmt.Printf("ID: %d, Name: %s, Email: %s\n", id, name, email)
    }
}
```

7.2.4 Update Data (UPDATE)

go

```go
func updateUser(db *sql.DB, id int, newEmail string) {
    query := "UPDATE users SET email = $1 WHERE id = $2"
    _, err := db.Exec(query, newEmail, id)
```

103

```go
    if err != nil {
        panic(err)
    }
    fmt.Println("User updated successfully!")
}
```

7.2.5 Delete Data (DELETE)

go

```go
func deleteUser(db *sql.DB, id int) {
    query := "DELETE FROM users WHERE id = $1"
    _, err := db.Exec(query, id)
    if err != nil {
        panic(err)
    }
    fmt.Println("User deleted successfully!")
}
```

7.3 Using ORM Libraries Like GORM

7.3.1 Installing GORM

sh

```sh
go get gorm.io/gorm
go get gorm.io/driver/postgres  # For PostgreSQL
```

```
go get gorm.io/driver/mysql      # For MySQL
```

7.3.2 Connecting to the Database Using GORM

PostgreSQL Connection

go

```go
package main

import (
    "fmt"
    "gorm.io/driver/postgres"
    "gorm.io/gorm"
)

const dsn = "host=localhost user=postgres
password=yourpassword dbname=testdb port=5432
sslmode=disable"

func main() {
    db, err := gorm.Open(postgres.Open(dsn),
&gorm.Config{})
    if err != nil {
        panic(err)
    }

    fmt.Println("Connected to PostgreSQL using
GORM!")
```

```
}
```

MySQL Connection

go

```
const                dsn              =
"root:yourpassword@tcp(127.0.0.1:3306)/testdb?c
harset=utf8mb4&parseTime=True&loc=Local"
db,     err    :=     gorm.Open(mysql.Open(dsn),
&gorm.Config{})
```

7.3.3 Defining a Model

go

```
type User struct {
    ID     uint   `gorm:"primaryKey"`
    Name   string `gorm:"size:100"`
    Email  string `gorm:"unique"`
}
```

7.3.4 Auto-Migrate Tables

go

```
db.AutoMigrate(&User{})
```

7.3.5 CRUD Operations with GORM

Create a New User

go

```
db.Create(&User{Name:      "Alice",      Email:
"alice@example.com"})
```

Read Users

go

```
var users []User
db.Find(&users)
fmt.Println(users)
```

Update a User

go

```
db.Model(&User{}).Where("id      =      ?",
1).Update("Email", "newemail@example.com")
```

Delete a User

go

```
db.Delete(&User{}, 1)
```

7.4 Summary

Concept	Description
Connecting to PostgreSQL & MySQL	Using `sql.Open()` and drivers.
Performing CRUD Operations	`Exec()`, `Query()`, and `QueryRow()`.
Using GORM	ORM library for easier database handling.

Next Chapter: Authentication and Security in Go

In the next chapter, we will:

- Implement **JWT authentication**.
- Use **bcrypt for password hashing**.
- Follow **best security practices** for Go applications.

CHAPTER 8

AUTHENTICATION AND SECURITY IN GO

Security is a **critical** part of backend development, ensuring that user data remains **safe** and **protected** from unauthorized access. In this chapter, we will cover:

- **Implementing JWT authentication** for secure API access.
- **Secure password hashing with bcrypt** to store passwords safely.
- **Best practices for API security** to prevent common vulnerabilities.

8.1 Implementing JWT Authentication

8.1.1 What is JWT?

JSON Web Tokens (JWT) are used for **user authentication** and **authorization** in web applications. JWT consists of:

1. **Header** – Specifies the algorithm used (e.g., HS256).
2. **Payload** – Contains claims (user information, expiration time, etc.).
3. **Signature** – Verifies the token's integrity.

8.1.2 Installing JWT Package

Install the `github.com/golang-jwt/jwt/v4` package:

sh

```sh
go get github.com/golang-jwt/jwt/v4
```

8.1.3 Generating JWT Tokens

go

```go
package main

import (
    "fmt"
    "time"
    "github.com/golang-jwt/jwt/v4"
)

var jwtKey = []byte("my_secret_key")
```

```go
func generateToken(username string) (string,
error) {
    token                          :=
jwt.NewWithClaims(jwt.SigningMethodHS256,
jwt.MapClaims{
        "username": username,
        "exp":        time.Now().Add(time.Hour *
1).Unix(), // Token expires in 1 hour
    })
    return token.SignedString(jwtKey)
}

func main() {
    token, err := generateToken("Alice")
    if err != nil {
        panic(err)
    }
    fmt.Println("Generated Token:", token)
}
```

Explanation

- **jwt.NewWithClaims** creates a token with a username and expiration time.
- **jwt.SigningMethodHS256** secures the token with a secret key.
- **SignedString(jwtKey)** signs the token using the secret key.

8.1.4 Verifying JWT Tokens

go

```
func       verifyToken(tokenString       string)
(*jwt.Token, error) {
    return    jwt.Parse(tokenString,    func(token
*jwt.Token) (interface{}, error) {
        return jwtKey, nil
    })
}
```

8.2 Secure Password Hashing with bcrypt

Storing passwords **in plain text** is insecure. Instead, we **hash passwords** using bcrypt.

8.2.1 Installing bcrypt

sh

```
go get golang.org/x/crypto/bcrypt
```

8.2.2 Hashing Passwords

```go
go

package main

import (
    "fmt"
    "golang.org/x/crypto/bcrypt"
)

func hashPassword(password string) (string,
error) {
    hashedPassword, err :=
bcrypt.GenerateFromPassword([]byte(password),
bcrypt.DefaultCost)
    return string(hashedPassword), err
}

func main() {
    hashed, _ := hashPassword("securepassword")
    fmt.Println("Hashed Password:", hashed)
}
```

Explanation

- **bcrypt.GenerateFromPassword** hashes the password using a strong algorithm.
- **bcrypt.DefaultCost** ensures a good balance between security and performance.

8.2.3 Verifying Passwords

go

```go
func checkPassword(hashedPassword, password string) bool {
    err := bcrypt.CompareHashAndPassword([]byte(hashedPassword), []byte(password))
    return err == nil
}
```

8.3 Best Practices for API Security

8.3.1 Use HTTPS

- Always encrypt API communication with **HTTPS**.

8.3.2 Secure API Endpoints

- Use **JWT authentication** to protect routes.
- Restrict access to sensitive endpoints.

8.3.3 Rate Limiting

- Prevent brute force attacks by limiting API requests.

8.3.4 Avoid Storing Sensitive Data in JWT

- Never store **passwords** or **sensitive information** inside JWT payloads.

8.4 Summary

Concept	Description
JWT Authentication	Used for securing API endpoints.
bcrypt Hashing	Encrypts passwords before storage.
API Security Practices	**Best** HTTPS, rate limiting, and secure data storage.

Next Chapter: Handling Concurrent Requests in Go

In the next chapter, we will:

- **Understand concurrency in Go** with Goroutines.
- **Use channels for safe communication between threads.**
- **Build high-performance concurrent APIs.**

CHAPTER 9

HANDLING CONCURRENT REQUESTS IN GO

Concurrency is one of **Go's strongest features**, allowing developers to handle multiple tasks efficiently. This chapter will cover:

- **Concurrency vs. parallelism**
- **Using Goroutines and channels**
- **Real-world example: Handling multiple API requests concurrently**

9.1 Concurrency vs. Parallelism

Concurrency and parallelism are **not the same** but are often confused.

Concept	Definition
Concurrency	Multiple tasks start and make progress at the same time, but not necessarily executing at the exact same moment.

Concept	Definition
Parallelism	Multiple tasks execute at the exact same time, using multiple processors or cores.

9.1.1 Example of Concurrency

- A Go web server handling multiple requests **one at a time** but switching between them.

9.1.2 Example of Parallelism

- A machine learning application using **multiple CPU cores** to train a model faster.

 Go focuses on concurrency but can achieve parallelism when multiple CPU cores are available.

9.2 Using Goroutines and Channels

Goroutines allow **concurrent execution** of functions.

9.2.1 Creating a Goroutine

A **Goroutine** is a lightweight thread in Go.

```go
go

package main

import (
    "fmt"
    "time"
)

func printMessage(msg string) {
    for i := 0; i < 5; i++ {
        fmt.Println(msg)
        time.Sleep(time.Millisecond * 500)
    }
}

func main() {
    go printMessage("Hello from Goroutine!") // Run concurrently
    printMessage("Hello from Main function!") // Runs normally
}
```

Explanation

- `go printMessage("Hello from Goroutine!")` starts a **new Goroutine**.
- **The program may exit before the Goroutine finishes!** (because the main function does not wait).

9.2.2 Synchronizing with WaitGroup

To prevent the program from exiting before Goroutines finish, use **sync.WaitGroup**.

```go
package main

import (
    "fmt"
    "sync"
    "time"
)

func        printMessage(msg        string,        wg
*sync.WaitGroup) {
    defer wg.Done() // Mark task as done
    for i := 0; i < 5; i++ {
        fmt.Println(msg)
        time.Sleep(time.Millisecond * 500)
    }
}

func main() {
    var wg sync.WaitGroup
    wg.Add(2) // We have 2 Goroutines
```

```go
go printMessage("Goroutine 1", &wg)
go printMessage("Goroutine 2", &wg)

wg.Wait()  // Wait for all Goroutines to
finish
fmt.Println("All Goroutines finished!")
}
```

Best Practice: Always use `WaitGroup` when managing multiple Goroutines.

9.2.3 Using Channels for Communication

Goroutines communicate using **channels**.

```go

package main

import "fmt"

func sendMessage(ch chan string) {
    ch <- "Hello from Goroutine!"
}

func main() {
```

```
messageChannel := make(chan string)
go sendMessage(messageChannel)

message := <-messageChannel // Receiving data
from channel
fmt.Println(message)
}
```

Explanation

- `ch <- "Hello"` **sends** data into the channel.
- `<-ch` **receives** data from the channel.

Why Use Channels?

- Avoids **race conditions** in shared memory.
- Ensures **safe data exchange** between Goroutines.

9.2.4 Buffered vs. Unbuffered Channels

- **Unbuffered Channels** – Block until data is received.
- **Buffered Channels** – Allow storing multiple messages.

Example: Buffered Channel

```
go
```

```
ch := make(chan string, 2) // Capacity of 2
```

121

```
ch <- "Hello"
ch <- "World"

fmt.Println(<-ch) // Output: Hello
fmt.Println(<-ch) // Output: World
```

9.3 Real-World Example: Handling Multiple API Requests Concurrently

A common use case is handling **multiple API requests** concurrently.

9.3.1 Simulating API Requests with Goroutines

```go
package main

import (
    "fmt"
    "net/http"
    "sync"
    "time"
)

var urls = []string{

"https://jsonplaceholder.typicode.com/todos/1",
```

```
    "https://jsonplaceholder.typicode.com/todos/2",

    "https://jsonplaceholder.typicode.com/todos/3",
}

func fetchData(url string, wg *sync.WaitGroup) {
    defer wg.Done()
    start := time.Now()

    resp, err := http.Get(url)
    if err != nil {
        fmt.Println("Error fetching:", url)
        return
    }
    defer resp.Body.Close()

    fmt.Printf("Fetched   %s   in   %v\n",   url,
time.Since(start))
}

func main() {
    var wg sync.WaitGroup
    for _, url := range urls {
        wg.Add(1)
        go fetchData(url, &wg)
    }
    wg.Wait()
    fmt.Println("All API requests completed!")
```

```
}
```

How It Works

- `fetchData()` makes an **HTTP request** in a Goroutine.
- `sync.WaitGroup` ensures **all API calls finish** before the program exits.

Advantage: Reduces API response time by running multiple requests **concurrently**.

9.4 Summary

Concept	Description
Goroutines	Lightweight threads for concurrency.
WaitGroup	Synchronizes multiple Goroutines.
Channels	Facilitates safe data exchange.
Buffered vs. Unbuffered	Buffered stores multiple values, unbuffered blocks until received.
Concurrent API Requests	Improves performance by making multiple API calls in parallel.

Next Chapter: Logging and Debugging in Go

In the next chapter, we will:

- **Use logging for debugging Go applications.**
- **Monitor API performance.**
- **Understand error handling in production.**

CHAPTER 10

LOGGING AND DEBUGGING IN GO

Logging and debugging are **crucial** for understanding and fixing issues in Go applications. This chapter covers:

- **Logging with log and zap**
- **Debugging Go applications**
- **Error handling best practices**

10.1 Logging with log and zap

10.1.1 Using the Built-in log Package

Go's standard **log** package provides simple logging.

Basic Logging

go

```go
package main

import (
    "log"
```

```
)

func main() {
    log.Println("This is a basic log message.")
}
```

Output:

```
swift
```

```
2025/03/02 12:00:00 This is a basic log message.
```

10.1.2 Adding Timestamps

```
go
```

```
log.SetFlags(log.Ldate | log.Ltime |
log.Lshortfile)
log.Println("Log with timestamp and file
details")
```

Output:

```
pgsql
```

```
2025/03/02 12:00:00 main.go:8: Log with timestamp
and file details
```

10.1.3 Writing Logs to a File

```go
go

package main

import (
    "log"
    "os"
)

func main() {
    file, err := os.OpenFile("app.log",
os.O_APPEND|os.O_CREATE|os.O_WRONLY, 0666)
    if err != nil {
        log.Fatal(err)
    }
    defer file.Close()

    log.SetOutput(file)
    log.Println("This message is logged to a
file.")
}
```

10.1.4 Using `zap` for Structured Logging

`zap` is a **high-performance** logging library.

Install zap

```sh

go get go.uber.org/zap
```

Basic Usage

```go

package main

import (
    "go.uber.org/zap"
)

func main() {
    logger, _ := zap.NewProduction()
    defer logger.Sync()

    logger.Info("Structured logging with zap",
        zap.String("module", "auth"),
        zap.Int("user_id", 123),
    )
}
```

Output:

```json
```

```
{"level":"info","ts":1709467200,"msg":"Structur
ed                logging                with
zap","module":"auth","user_id":123}
```

Using zap with a Custom Logger

go

```
logger := zap.NewExample()
logger.Warn("Something        went        wrong!",
zap.String("module", "payment"))
```

10.2 Debugging Go Applications

Debugging helps in **identifying and fixing** issues quickly.

10.2.1 Using `fmt.Println()` for Quick Debugging

go

```
func main() {
    user := "Alice"
    fmt.Println("Debugging User:", user)
}
```

Best for: Small programs and quick checks.

10.2.2 Using `log.Println()` for More Details

```go
log.Println("Fetching user data from API...")
```

Best for: Debugging API calls and database queries.

10.2.3 Using pprof for Performance Debugging

pprof helps find **CPU and memory bottlenecks**.

Install pprof

```sh
go get net/http/pprof
```

Enable Profiling in Your Application

```go
import _ "net/http/pprof"

go func() {

log.Println(http.ListenAndServe("localhost:6060", nil))
}()
```

Run profiling tool:

sh

```
go                  tool                pprof
http://localhost:6060/debug/pprof/profile
```

10.3 Error Handling Best Practices

Error handling in Go is **explicit**, making it easier to debug.

10.3.1 Returning Errors from Functions

go

```go
func divide(a, b float64) (float64, error) {
    if b == 0 {
        return 0, fmt.Errorf("cannot divide by
zero")
    }
    return a / b, nil
}
```

10.3.2 Using `errors.Wrap()` for Context

Install `pkg/errors`:

sh

132

```
go get github.com/pkg/errors
go

import "github.com/pkg/errors"

func openFile(filename string) error {
    _, err := os.Open(filename)
    if err != nil {
        return errors.Wrap(err, "failed to open
file")
    }
    return nil
}
```

Best Practice: Always **wrap** errors with context.

10.4 Summary

Concept	Description
log package	Basic logging with timestamps and file logging.
zap logging	High-performance structured logging.
Debugging techniques	fmt.Println(), log.Println(), and pprof for performance analysis.

Concept	Description
Error handling	Return errors explicitly and use `errors.Wrap()` for context.

Next Chapter: Deploying Go Applications

In the next chapter, we will:

- **Containerize a Go app with Docker.**
- **Deploy it to Kubernetes and AWS.**
- **Optimize API performance for production.**

PART 3

GO FOR CLOUD COMPUTING

CHAPTER 11

INTRODUCTION TO CLOUD DEVELOPMENT WITH GO

Cloud computing has transformed how applications are built, deployed, and scaled. **Go** is an excellent choice for cloud development because of its **performance, concurrency support, and simplicity**. This chapter will cover:

- **Why Go is ideal for cloud applications**
- **Overview of cloud service providers (AWS, GCP, Azure)**
- **Deploying a simple Go app to the cloud**

11.1 Why Go is Ideal for Cloud Applications

Go was designed with **efficiency and scalability** in mind, making it a perfect fit for cloud computing.

11.1.1 Key Advantages of Go for Cloud Development

Feature	Benefit in Cloud Computing
Concurrency	Goroutines handle multiple tasks efficiently (e.g., API calls, background jobs).
Compiled Binary	Produces lightweight executables with no external dependencies.
Cross-Platform	Runs on Windows, Linux, macOS, and ARM-based architectures.
Fast Startup	Ideal for containerized applications and microservices.
Memory Efficiency	Optimized garbage collection minimizes cloud resource costs.

Use Cases:

- **Scalable APIs**: Microservices architectures.
- **Cloud Functions**: Serverless execution (AWS Lambda, Google Cloud Functions).
- **Infrastructure Automation**: Kubernetes controllers and CLI tools.

11.2 Overview of Cloud Service Providers (AWS, GCP, Azure)

Go is supported by **all major cloud providers**.

11.2.1 Amazon Web Services (AWS)

- **Best for:** Large-scale applications, microservices, serverless computing.
- **Go Support:**
    - **AWS Lambda** (Serverless Functions)
    - **EC2** (Compute Instances)
    - **S3** (Storage)
    - **DynamoDB** (NoSQL Database)
    - **Fargate & ECS** (Containerized Apps)

Install AWS SDK for Go:

sh

```
go get github.com/aws/aws-sdk-go
```

11.2.2 Google Cloud Platform (GCP)

- **Best for:** AI/ML workloads, cloud-native applications, Kubernetes.

- **Go Support:**
  - **Google App Engine** (Fully managed serverless platform)
  - **Cloud Run** (Container-based execution)
  - **Cloud Functions** (Event-driven serverless computing)
  - **Firestore** (NoSQL Database)

Install GCP SDK for Go:

sh

```
go get cloud.google.com/go
```

11.2.3 Microsoft Azure

- **Best for:** Enterprise applications, hybrid cloud solutions.
- **Go Support:**
  - **Azure Functions** (Serverless execution)
  - **Azure Kubernetes Service (AKS)** (Managed Kubernetes)
  - **Blob Storage** (Object Storage)

Install Azure SDK for Go:

sh

```
go get github.com/Azure/azure-sdk-for-go
```

11.3 Deploying a Simple Go App to the Cloud

Let's deploy a **basic Go web server** to the cloud.

11.3.1 Writing a Simple Go Web App

Create a new directory for your project:

```sh

mkdir go-cloud-app && cd go-cloud-app
```

Initialize a Go module:

```sh

go mod init go-cloud-app
```

Create a **main.go** file:

```go

package main

import (
    "fmt"
    "net/http"
```

```
    "os"
)


func    handler(w        http.ResponseWriter,    r
*http.Request) {
    fmt.Fprintln(w, "Hello, Cloud!")
}


func main() {
    port := os.Getenv("PORT") // Cloud providers
assign a port dynamically
    if port == "" {
        port = "8080" // Default for local
testing
    }

    http.HandleFunc("/", handler)
    fmt.Println("Server running on port:", port)
    http.ListenAndServe(":"+port, nil)
}
```

11.3.2 Deploying to AWS (Elastic Beanstalk)

1. **Install AWS CLI & Elastic Beanstalk CLI**

```sh
aws configure
```

141

2. **Initialize an Elastic Beanstalk application**

```sh
eb init -p go go-cloud-app
```

3. **Deploy**

```sh
eb create go-cloud-env
```

Elastic Beanstalk handles scaling and load balancing automatically.

11.3.3 Deploying to Google Cloud Run

1. **Authenticate Google Cloud CLI**

```sh
gcloud auth login
gcloud config set project YOUR_PROJECT_ID
```

2. **Build and push the container**

```sh
```

```
gcloud       builds      submit      --tag
gcr.io/YOUR_PROJECT_ID/go-cloud-app
```

3. **Deploy**

```
sh
```

```
gcloud  run  deploy  go-cloud-app  --image
gcr.io/YOUR_PROJECT_ID/go-cloud-app    --
platform managed
```

Cloud Run auto-scales the app based on demand.

11.3.4 Deploying to Azure App Service

1. **Login and create an App Service**

```
sh
```

```
az login
az  webapp  create  --resource-group
MyResourceGroup --plan MyPlan --name go-
cloud-app --runtime "GO|1.16"
```

2. **Deploy using Git**

```
sh
```

143

```
git init
git add .
git commit -m "Initial commit"
git          push          https://go-cloud-
app.scm.azurewebsites.net/go-cloud-
app.git master
```

Azure App Service provides automatic scaling and easy integration with Azure DevOps.

11.4 Summary

Concept	Description
Why Go for Cloud	Fast, efficient, concurrency-friendly.
Cloud Providers	AWS, GCP, Azure fully support Go applications.
Deployment Methods	Elastic Beanstalk, Cloud Run, Azure App Service.

Next Chapter: Building Serverless Applications with Go

In the next chapter, we will:

- **Deploy Go functions on AWS Lambda, Google Cloud Functions, and Azure Functions.**
- **Understand event-driven architecture.**
- **Optimize serverless performance.**

CHAPTER 12

BUILDING SERVERLESS APPLICATIONS WITH GO

Serverless computing enables developers to build applications without managing infrastructure. **Go** is an excellent choice for **serverless applications** due to its **low memory footprint, fast execution speed, and efficient concurrency management**.

In this chapter, we will cover:

- **Understanding serverless computing**
- **Using AWS Lambda with Go**
- **Building a real-world serverless API with Go and DynamoDB**

12.1 Understanding Serverless Computing

12.1.1 What is Serverless Computing?

Serverless computing allows developers to **run functions on-demand** without provisioning or managing servers.

Cloud providers dynamically allocate resources and scale automatically.

12.1.2 Benefits of Serverless Computing

Feature	Benefit
No server management	No need to manage servers, networking, or scaling.
Auto-scaling	Cloud providers automatically scale based on traffic.
Cost-efficient	Pay only for the time your function runs.
Event-driven	Functions trigger based on events (HTTP requests, database updates, etc.).

Common Use Cases:

- REST APIs
- Event-driven applications
- Data processing
- Chatbots & IoT applications

12.2 Using AWS Lambda with Go

AWS Lambda is a **serverless compute service** that runs Go functions in response to **HTTP requests, database changes, or other AWS events**.

12.2.1 Installing AWS Lambda Go SDK

Install the **AWS Lambda Go package**:

```sh
go get github.com/aws/aws-lambda-go/lambda
```

12.2.2 Writing a Simple AWS Lambda Function

Create a file `main.go`:

```go
package main

import (
    "context"
    "fmt"
    "github.com/aws/aws-lambda-go/lambda"
)
```

```go
// Lambda function handler
func handler(ctx context.Context, name string)
(string, error) {
    return fmt.Sprintf("Hello, %s!", name), nil
}

func main() {
    lambda.Start(handler)
}
```

12.2.3 Building and Deploying to AWS Lambda

1. **Build the executable for AWS Lambda**:

   sh

   ```sh
   GOOS=linux GOARCH=amd64 go build -o main
   main.go
   zip function.zip main
   ```

2. **Deploy to AWS Lambda using AWS CLI**:

   sh

   ```sh
   aws lambda create-function --function-name
   GoLambdaFunction \
       --runtime      go1.x      --role
   arn:aws:iam::YOUR_ACCOUNT_ID:role/YOUR_LA
   MBDA_ROLE \
   ```

149

```
--handler      main      --zip-file
fileb://function.zip
```

3. **Invoke the function**:

```sh
sh
```

```
aws   lambda   invoke   --function-name
GoLambdaFunction response.json
```

12.3 Real-World Example: Serverless API with Go and DynamoDB

12.3.1 Installing DynamoDB SDK for Go

```sh
sh
```

```
go        get        github.com/aws/aws-sdk-go-
v2/service/dynamodb
```

12.3.2 Creating a Simple Serverless API

We will build a **serverless API** that stores user data in DynamoDB.

12.3.2.1 Define the Go Struct for Users

```go
go
```

```go
type User struct {
    ID    string `json:"id"`
    Name  string `json:"name"`
    Email string `json:"email"`
}
```

12.3.2.2 Writing the Lambda Function to Store Data

go

```go
package main

import (
    "context"
    "encoding/json"
    "fmt"
    "github.com/aws/aws-lambda-go/events"
    "github.com/aws/aws-lambda-go/lambda"
    "github.com/aws/aws-sdk-go-v2/aws"
    "github.com/aws/aws-sdk-go-v2/config"
    "github.com/aws/aws-sdk-go-
v2/service/dynamodb"
    "github.com/aws/aws-sdk-go-
v2/service/dynamodb/types"
)

type User struct {
    ID    string `json:"id"`
    Name  string `json:"name"`
```

151

```go
    Email string `json:"email"`
}


var dbClient *dynamodb.Client


func init() {
    cfg,              err               :=
config.LoadDefaultConfig(context.TODO())
    if err != nil {
        panic(fmt.Sprintf("unable   to   load   SDK
config, %v", err))
    }
    dbClient = dynamodb.NewFromConfig(cfg)
}


func   handler(ctx    context.Context,   request
events.APIGatewayProxyRequest)
(events.APIGatewayProxyResponse, error) {
    var user User
    err := json.Unmarshal([]byte(request.Body),
&user)
    if err != nil {
        return
events.APIGatewayProxyResponse{StatusCode:  400,
Body: "Invalid request"}, nil
    }


    _,      err      =       dbClient.PutItem(ctx,
&dynamodb.PutItemInput{
```

```
        TableName: aws.String("Users"),
        Item: map[string]types.AttributeValue{
            "id":
&types.AttributeValueMemberS{Value: user.ID},
            "name":
&types.AttributeValueMemberS{Value: user.Name},
            "email":
&types.AttributeValueMemberS{Value: user.Email},
        },
    })

    if err != nil {
        return
events.APIGatewayProxyResponse{StatusCode:  500,
Body: "Error storing user"}, nil
    }

    return
events.APIGatewayProxyResponse{StatusCode:  200,
Body: "User stored successfully"}, nil
}

func main() {
    lambda.Start(handler)
}
```

12.3.3 Deploying the API to AWS

1. **Create a DynamoDB table**:

sh

```
aws dynamodb create-table --table-name
Users \
    --attribute-definitions
AttributeName=id,AttributeType=S \
    --key-schema
AttributeName=id,KeyType=HASH \
    --provisioned-throughput
ReadCapacityUnits=1,WriteCapacityUnits=1
```

2. **Build and package the Lambda function**:

sh

```
GOOS=linux GOARCH=amd64 go build -o main
main.go
zip function.zip main
```

3. **Deploy to AWS Lambda**:

sh

```
aws lambda create-function --function-name
StoreUserFunction \
    --runtime        go1.x        --role
arn:aws:iam::YOUR_ACCOUNT_ID:role/YOUR_LA
MBDA_ROLE \
```

154

```
--handler      main      --zip-file
fileb://function.zip
```

4. **Expose the function via API Gateway**:

```sh

aws apigateway create-rest-api --name "Go
Serverless API"
```

5. **Invoke the API** using CURL:

```sh

curl -X POST https://your-api-gateway-
url.com/users \
    -H "Content-Type: application/json" \
    -d    '{"id":"1",    "name":"Alice",
"email":"alice@example.com"}'
```

12.4 Summary

Concept	Description
Serverless Computing	Run functions without managing infrastructure.

Concept	Description
AWS Lambda with Go	Deploy Go functions on AWS Lambda.
DynamoDB Integration	Store and retrieve data in a NoSQL database.
Building a Serverless API	Implemented API with AWS Lambda & DynamoDB.

Next Chapter: Containerization with Docker and Go

In the next chapter, we will:

- **Containerize a Go application using Docker**
- **Understand Docker Compose for multi-container setups**
- **Deploy a containerized Go app to AWS and Kubernetes**

CHAPTER 13:

CONTAINERIZATION WITH

DOCKER AND GO

Containerization is a key technology for **deploying and scaling applications** in modern cloud environments. **Docker** allows you to package a Go application with all its dependencies, making it **portable, lightweight, and scalable**.

This chapter will cover:

- **Why Docker?**
- **Writing Dockerfiles for Go applications**
- **Running Go apps in Docker containers**

13.1 Why Docker?

Docker simplifies application deployment by **packaging everything** needed to run an app into a single container.

13.1.1 Key Benefits of Docker

Feature	Benefit
Portability	Runs consistently across different environments (local, staging, production).
Isolation	Ensures dependencies don't conflict between apps.
Scalability	Works seamlessly with Kubernetes for scaling microservices.
Efficiency	Lightweight alternative to virtual machines (VMs).

Use Cases:

- Running Go applications in **development, testing, and production** environments.
- Deploying Go applications as **microservices**.
- Ensuring **consistent** builds across teams.

13.2 Writing Dockerfiles for Go Applications

A **Dockerfile** is a script that automates the **containerization** of an application.

13.2.1 Installing Docker

If Docker is not installed, download it from:
👈 https://www.docker.com/get-started

Verify installation:

```sh
```

```
docker --version
```

13.2.2 Creating a Basic Go Web App

Create a new project directory:

```sh
```

```
mkdir go-docker-app && cd go-docker-app
```

Initialize a **Go module**:

```sh
```

```
go mod init go-docker-app
```

Create a main.go file:

```go
```

```
package main
```

159

```go
import (
    "fmt"
    "net/http"
    "os"
)

func    handler(w    http.ResponseWriter,    r
*http.Request) {
    fmt.Fprintf(w, "Hello, Dockerized Go App!")
}

func main() {
    port := os.Getenv("PORT")
    if port == "" {
        port = "8080"
    }

    http.HandleFunc("/", handler)
    fmt.Println("Server running on port:", port)
    http.ListenAndServe(":"+port, nil)
}
```

13.2.3 Writing the Dockerfile

Create a file named **Dockerfile** in the project directory.

```
dockerfile
```

160

```
# Use the official Go image
FROM golang:1.20 AS builder

# Set the working directory
WORKDIR /app

#  go.mod and go.sum, then download dependencies
 go.mod go.sum ./
RUN go mod download

#  the rest of the application code
 . .

# Build the Go application
RUN go build -o main .

# Use a minimal image for final container
FROM alpine:latest
WORKDIR /root/

#  the compiled Go binary
 --from=builder /app/main .

# Expose the application port
EXPOSE 8080

# Run the application
CMD ["./main"]
```

Explanation of the Dockerfile

Step	Description
`FROM golang:1.20 AS builder`	Uses the **official Go image** as the build environment.
`WORKDIR /app`	Sets the working directory inside the container.
`go.mod go.sum ./`	Copies dependency files for efficient caching.
`RUN go mod download`	Downloads dependencies before ing the full code.
`. .`	Copies the rest of the application files.
`RUN go build -o main .`	Builds the Go binary.
`FROM alpine:latest`	Uses a **lightweight Alpine Linux image** for the final container.
`--from=builder /app/main .`	Copies the compiled binary from the builder stage.

Step	Description
EXPOSE 8080	Informs Docker that the container will use **port 8080**.
CMD ["./main"]	Runs the compiled Go application.

13.3 Running Go Apps in Docker Containers

13.3.1 Building and Running the Container

Build the Docker image:

```sh

docker build -t go-docker-app .
```

Run the container:

```sh

docker run -p 8080:8080 go-docker-app
```

Test   the   application:
Open   **http://localhost:8080**   in   your   browser.
Output:

```
Hello, Dockerized Go App!
```

13.3.2 Running in Detached Mode

To run the container **in the background**:

sh

```
docker run -d -p 8080:8080 go-docker-app
```

Check running containers:

sh

```
docker ps
```

Stop the container:

sh

```
docker stop <container_id>
```

13.3.3 Using Docker Compose for Multi-Container Apps

If your Go application requires **a database (PostgreSQL, MySQL, MongoDB, etc.)**, use **Docker Compose**.

Create a **docker-compose.yml** file:

```yaml
version: "3.8"

services:
  app:
    build: .
    ports:
      - "8080:8080"
    environment:
      PORT: 8080
    depends_on:
      - db

  db:
    image: postgres:latest
    environment:
      POSTGRES_USER: user
      POSTGRES_PASSWORD: password
      POSTGRES_DB: mydatabase
    ports:
      - "5432:5432"
```

Run the entire setup:

165

```sh
docker-compose up -d
```

Docker Compose allows running multiple services together.

13.3.4 Pushing the Image to Docker Hub

Login to Docker Hub:

```sh
docker login
```

Tag the image:

```sh
docker tag go-docker-app username/go-docker-app
```

3 Push the image:

```sh
docker push username/go-docker-app
```

Now, anyone can pull and run your app:

sh

```
docker pull username/go-docker-app
docker run -p 8080:8080 username/go-docker-app
```

13.4 Summary

Concept	Description
Why Docker?	Portability, isolation, efficiency.
Dockerfile	Defines how to containerize a Go application.
Running Containers	`docker build`, `docker run`, `docker-compose`.
Multi-Container Apps	Use **Docker Compose** for apps with databases.
Deploying to Docker Hub	`docker push` allows easy sharing of images.

Next Chapter: Deploying Go Applications with Kubernetes

In the next chapter, we will:

- **Deploy a Go application to Kubernetes**
- **Use Kubernetes services for scaling**
- **Manage deployments with `kubectl`**

CHAPTER 14

DEPLOYING GO APPLICATIONS WITH KUBERNETES

Kubernetes is an open-source platform designed to **automate** the deployment, scaling, and management of containerized applications. It is a powerful tool for managing **microservices** and applications in **production environments**. This chapter will cover:

- **Introduction to Kubernetes**
- **Setting up a Go microservice in Kubernetes**
- **Managing Kubernetes pods and services**

14.1 Introduction to Kubernetes

14.1.1 What is Kubernetes?

Kubernetes (K8s) is a **container orchestration** tool that helps you manage containers, automate deployments, scaling, and networking. It provides a unified API to interact with your application, making it easier to manage large-scale microservices and distributed systems.

Key Concepts in Kubernetes:

Concept	Description
Pod	A pod is the **smallest deployable unit** in Kubernetes and can contain one or more containers.
Service	A service exposes a set of **pods** and provides a stable endpoint for accessing them.
Deployment	Manages the **replicas** of a pod and ensures the desired state (number of replicas) is maintained.
Namespace	A way to organize resources into separate groups for multi-tenancy or isolation.
Kubernetes Cluster	A set of **worker nodes** that run your containerized applications.

14.1.2 Why Kubernetes for Go Applications?

- **Scalability**: Easily scale up or down based on traffic or demand.
- **Resilience**: Automatically restarts failed containers and reschedules pods.

- **Service Discovery**: Automatically assigns DNS names to services and load balances traffic between pods.

14.2 Setting Up a Go Microservice in Kubernetes

Let's walk through the steps to deploy a **simple Go microservice** using Kubernetes.

14.2.1 Writing a Simple Go Microservice

1. Create a **Go microservice** that runs an HTTP server (similar to previous examples).

```go
package main

import (
    "fmt"
    "net/http"
    "os"
)

func handler(w http.ResponseWriter, r *http.Request) {
    fmt.Fprintf(w, "Hello, Kubernetes-powered Go App!")
```

```
}

func main() {
    port := os.Getenv("PORT")
    if port == "" {
        port = "8080"
    }

    http.HandleFunc("/", handler)
    fmt.Println("Server running on port:", port)
    http.ListenAndServe(":"+port, nil)
}
```

14.2.2 Writing a Dockerfile for the Go App

Create a **Dockerfile** to containerize the Go application.

dockerfile

```
# Step 1: Build the Go binary
FROM golang:1.20 AS builder

WORKDIR /app
 . .
RUN go mod tidy
RUN go build -o main .
```

```
# Step 2: Create a minimal image with the Go
binary
FROM alpine:latest

WORKDIR /root/
 --from=builder /app/main .
EXPOSE 8080
CMD ["./main"]
```

14.2.3 Building and Pushing the Docker Image

1. Build the image:

   sh

   ```
   docker build -t go-k8s-app .
   ```

2. Tag the image for Docker Hub:

   sh

   ```
   docker tag go-k8s-app username/go-k8s-app
   ```

3. Push the image to Docker Hub:

   sh

   ```
   docker push username/go-k8s-app
   ```

14.2.4 Deploying the Go Microservice to Kubernetes

To deploy a Go microservice, we will need to write a Kubernetes **Deployment** and **Service** definition.

14.2.4.1 Creating a Kubernetes Deployment YAML

yaml

```yaml
apiVersion: apps/v1
kind: Deployment
metadata:
  name: go-k8s-deployment
spec:
  replicas: 3
  selector:
    matchLabels:
      app: go-k8s-app
  template:
    metadata:
      labels:
        app: go-k8s-app
    spec:
      containers:
        - name: go-k8s-app
          image: username/go-k8s-app:latest
          ports:
            - containerPort: 8080
```

This `Deployment` will:

- Create 3 replicas of the Go microservice.
- Use the **Docker image** pushed earlier (`username/go-k8s-app:latest`).

14.2.4.2 Creating a Kubernetes Service YAML

yaml

```
apiVersion: v1
kind: Service
metadata:
  name: go-k8s-service
spec:
  selector:
    app: go-k8s-app
  ports:
    - protocol: TCP
      port: 8080
      targetPort: 8080
  type: LoadBalancer
```

This **Service** will:

- Expose the Go application on port 8080.
- Use a **LoadBalancer** to distribute incoming traffic across the pods.

14.2.5 Applying the Kubernetes Configuration

1. **Create the Deployment and Service:**

   sh

   ```
   kubectl apply -f go-k8s-deployment.yaml
   kubectl apply -f go-k8s-service.yaml
   ```

2. **Check the Deployment:**

   sh

   ```
   kubectl get deployments
   ```

3. **Check the Pods:**

   sh

   ```
   kubectl get pods
   ```

4. **Expose the Service** (if using Minikube or a local Kubernetes setup):

   sh

   ```
   kubectl expose deployment go-k8s-deployment --type=LoadBalancer --name=go-k8s-service
   ```

14.3 Managing Kubernetes Pods and Services

Once your Go application is deployed, you can manage Kubernetes pods and services with the following commands.

14.3.1 Managing Pods

Listing Pods

sh

```
kubectl get pods
```

Deleting a Pod

sh

```
kubectl delete pod <pod-name>
```

Kubernetes will automatically **replace** the deleted pod with a new one to maintain the desired state (as specified in the Deployment).

14.3.2 Scaling the Application

To scale the number of pods:

sh

```
kubectl scale deployment go-k8s-deployment --
replicas=5
```

14.3.3 Viewing Logs of a Pod

sh

```
kubectl logs <pod-name>
```

14.3.4 Exposing the Application with a Service

To make your application publicly accessible, expose it using a **Service**:

sh

```
kubectl expose deployment go-k8s-deployment --
type=LoadBalancer --name=go-k8s-service
```

If you're using a local Kubernetes environment like **Minikube**, you can also run:

sh

```
minikube service go-k8s-service
```

This will open the service in your default browser.

14.4 Summary

Concept	Description
Kubernetes	A platform for automating deployment, scaling, and management of containerized applications.
Deployment	A resource that manages the pods and ensures that the desired state is maintained.
Service	Exposes the pods to the network and provides load balancing.
Scaling	Kubernetes allows easy scaling of microservices by adjusting replicas.
Managing Pods and Services	Use `kubectl` to manage your pods and services in the cluster.

Next Chapter: Managing Kubernetes with Helm

In the next chapter, we will:

- **Learn Helm** for managing Kubernetes applications.
- **Create Helm charts** for deploying Go applications.
- **Simplify application deployment** with Helm templates.

CHAPTER 15

CLOUD-NATIVE DEVELOPMENT WITH GO

Cloud-native development focuses on creating applications that are designed to run in dynamic and scalable cloud environments. **Go** is a great choice for building **cloud-native applications** due to its **efficiency, simplicity, and strong concurrency support**.

In this chapter, we will cover:

- **Using Go for cloud-native applications**
- **Implementing cloud-based event-driven architectures**
- **Real-world example: Building a scalable cloud-based chat app**

15.1 Using Go for Cloud-Native Applications

15.1.1 What are Cloud-Native Applications?

Cloud-native applications are designed to take full advantage of the **cloud computing model** by being:

- **Microservices-based**: Small, independently deployable services.
- **Event-driven**: Reacting to events (e.g., message queues, HTTP requests).
- **Scalable**: Automatically scaling up or down based on demand.
- **Resilient**: Able to recover from failures quickly.

15.1.2 Why Go for Cloud-Native Development?

Go is perfect for cloud-native applications because of:

- **Fast execution**: Low memory footprint and fast startup times.
- **Concurrency**: Goroutines make it easy to handle multiple tasks simultaneously (perfect for microservices).
- **Cross-platform**: Go applications can run on any cloud platform or container.

15.1.3 Cloud-Native Development Patterns

Pattern	Description
Microservices	Decompose applications into small, loosely-coupled services.

Pattern	Description
Event-Driven Architecture	Systems communicate via asynchronous events (e.g., messages, notifications).
Auto-Scaling	Automatically scale services in response to demand.
Service Discovery	Services automatically discover and communicate with each other.

15.2 Implementing Cloud-Based Event-Driven Architectures

15.2.1 What is Event-Driven Architecture?

Event-driven architecture (EDA) is a design pattern where services communicate via **events** (messages, notifications, etc.), rather than direct synchronous API calls. This pattern is common in **cloud-native** systems because it provides:

- **Loose coupling**: Services are independent and don't need to know the implementation details of other services.
- **Scalability**: Event-driven systems scale efficiently by reacting to incoming events.

182

- **Real-time processing**: Processes can react to events immediately when they occur.

15.2.2 Building Event-Driven Systems in Go

Go has excellent support for building **event-driven** systems using message brokers such as **RabbitMQ, Apache Kafka,** or **AWS SQS**. Here's an example of using **AWS SQS** to handle events in a Go application.

15.2.3 Integrating AWS SQS with Go for Event Processing

Step 1: Install AWS SDK for Go

sh

```
go get github.com/aws/aws-sdk-go-v2
go get github.com/aws/aws-sdk-go-v2/config
go get github.com/aws/aws-sdk-go-v2/service/sqs
```

Step 2: Sending Events to SQS Queue

go

```
package main

import (
    "context"
```

```
    "fmt"
    "log"
    "github.com/aws/aws-sdk-go-v2/aws"
    "github.com/aws/aws-sdk-go-v2/config"
    "github.com/aws/aws-sdk-go-v2/service/sqs"
)


func    sendMessageToQueue(queueURL,    message
string) error {
    cfg,                    err                    :=
config.LoadDefaultConfig(context.TODO())
    if err != nil {
        return err
    }

    svc := sqs.NewFromConfig(cfg)

    // Send message to the queue
    _,   err   =   svc.SendMessage(context.TODO(),
&sqs.SendMessageInput{
        QueueUrl:    &queueURL,
        MessageBody: aws.String(message),
    })

    if err != nil {
        return err
    }

    fmt.Println("Message sent successfully!")
```

184

```go
    return nil
}


func main() {
    queueURL      :=      "https://sqs.us-west-
2.amazonaws.com/your-account-id/your-queue-
name"
    message := "User message event"
    err := sendMessageToQueue(queueURL, message)
    if err != nil {
        log.Fatalf("Failed to send message: %v",
err)
    }
}
```

Step 3: Processing Events from the Queue

go

```go
func   receiveMessagesFromQueue(queueURL  string)
error {
    cfg,              err              :=
config.LoadDefaultConfig(context.TODO())
    if err != nil {
        return err
    }

    svc := sqs.NewFromConfig(cfg)
```

```go
    result,                     err                 :=
svc.ReceiveMessage(context.TODO(),
&sqs.ReceiveMessageInput{
        QueueUrl:               &queueURL,
        MaxNumberOfMessages: 10,
        WaitTimeSeconds:     20, // long polling
    })

    if err != nil {
        return err
    }

    for _, message := range result.Messages {
        fmt.Println("Received            message:",
*message.Body)
        // Process the event (e.g., store to
database)
    }

    return nil
}

func main() {
    queueURL       :=        "https://sqs.us-west-
2.amazonaws.com/your-account-id/your-queue-
name"
    err := receiveMessagesFromQueue(queueURL)
    if err != nil {
```

```
    log.Fatalf("Failed to receive messages:
%v", err)
    }
}
```

Explanation:

- The **sendMessageToQueue** function sends messages to an AWS SQS queue (event).
- The **receiveMessagesFromQueue** function listens for events from the queue and processes them (event handling).

This basic pattern allows you to build scalable and responsive systems that react to events in real time.

15.3 Real-World Example: Building a Scalable Cloud-Based Chat App

Let's build a simple **cloud-based chat application** that uses event-driven architecture and Go.

15.3.1 System Design

- **Frontend**: Web client or mobile app that sends and receives messages.

- **Backend**: Go-based microservices handle chat message storage, real-time delivery, and notifications.
- **Event Queue**: Use a message broker (like AWS SQS or RabbitMQ) to send messages and notifications between services.

15.3.2 High-Level Flow

1. **User sends a message** (via frontend).
2. **Backend microservice** receives the message, processes it, and **pushes it to the event queue**.
3. **Notification service** consumes events from the queue and sends notifications to users.
4. **Message storage** service stores the messages in a database (like DynamoDB or MongoDB).

15.3.3 Implementing the Chat App Backend in Go

Step 1: Setting up the Message Sending Microservice

The message sending microservice will:

- Accept incoming messages from clients.
- Place the message into the event queue (e.g., SQS).

Step 2: Real-Time Message Delivery

Using **WebSockets** or a similar protocol to push messages to clients as soon as they're received.

Step 3: Storing Chat Messages

Store chat messages in a **NoSQL database** (e.g., DynamoDB or MongoDB) for persistence.

15.3.4 Scaling the Chat Application

To scale the chat application:

- Use **multiple microservices** behind a load balancer (Kubernetes helps manage this).
- **Horizontal scaling** for services like notifications and message storage.
- **Auto-scaling** to handle high volumes of messages during peak usage.

15.4 Summary

Concept	Description
Cloud-Native Applications	Build scalable, resilient apps designed for the cloud.
Event-Driven Architecture	Use message queues to decouple services and enable asynchronous communication.
Go in Cloud-Native Apps	Go is ideal for building efficient, scalable cloud-based applications.
Scalable Cloud-Based Chat	Example of building a scalable chat app using Go and event-driven architecture.

Next Chapter: Microservices in Go and Kubernetes

In the next chapter, we will:

- **Architect a Go-based microservices system.**
- **Deploy microservices with Kubernetes.**
- **Implement service discovery, scaling, and management.**

CHAPTER 16

DJANGO MIDDLEWARE AND SECURITY BEST PRACTICES

Django, as a **high-level web framework**, offers a powerful set of tools to develop secure and performant web applications. One of its core features is **middleware**, which allows you to process requests and responses globally before reaching the views or after the response is processed. In this chapter, we will explore:

- **Understanding Django middleware**
- **Cross-Site Request Forgery (CSRF) and Clickjacking protection**
- **Security settings and performance optimizations**

16.1 Understanding Django Middleware

16.1.1 What is Middleware?

In Django, **middleware** is a framework of hooks that can process **requests** and **responses** globally. It is a lightweight, low-level plugin system that allows you to modify the request/response cycle.

16.1.2 How Middleware Works in Django

Middleware is executed in the following order:

1. **Request Handling**: Each middleware is called in the order specified in the `MIDDLEWARE` setting. It receives the HTTP request and either processes it or short-circuits the response cycle by returning a response.

2. **View Processing**: After middleware processes the request, the view is executed.

3. **Response Handling**: Once the view generates a response, middleware is invoked again in reverse order to modify the response before sending it to the client.

16.1.3 Common Use Cases for Middleware

- **Session management** (e.g., handling user sessions).
- **Authentication and authorization** (checking user permissions).
- **Cross-site scripting (XSS) filtering** (preventing malicious script execution).
- **Logging and debugging** (tracking requests and responses for debugging).

16.1.4 Writing Custom Middleware in Django

You can write custom middleware to handle specific functionality.

Example: Custom Middleware for Logging Requests

python

```python
from django.utils.timezone import localtime

class LogRequestMiddleware:
    def __init__(self, get_response):
        self.get_response = get_response

    def __call__(self, request):
        print(f"Request at {localtime()} - Method: {request.method}, Path: {request.path}")
        response = self.get_response(request)
        return response
```

Explanation:

- **__init__**: Initializes the middleware.
- **__call__**: The middleware intercepts requests, logs the request details, and passes it to the next middleware or view.

Adding Middleware to `settings.py`

python

```
MIDDLEWARE = [
    # Other middleware...
    'myapp.middleware.LogRequestMiddleware',    #
Add the custom middleware here
]
```

16.2 Cross-Site Request Forgery (CSRF) and Clickjacking
Protection

16.2.1 What is CSRF?

Cross-Site Request Forgery (CSRF) is a type of attack where an attacker tricks a user into performing actions they did not intend (e.g., submitting a form or changing account settings) by sending an authenticated request on behalf of the user.

Django has built-in protection to mitigate CSRF attacks through middleware.

16.2.2 CSRF Protection in Django

By default, Django comes with **CSRF middleware** enabled. The middleware works by checking that each form submission (or HTTP request) includes a **CSRF token**, which is unique to each session. If a request is made without a valid token, Django will reject it.

Adding CSRF Protection to Forms

In your template, you need to include the `{% csrf_token %}` tag in every form that submits data to the server.

html

```html
<form method="post">
    {% csrf_token %}
    <!-- Your form fields here -->
    <button type="submit">Submit</button>
</form>
```

Disabling CSRF Protection for Specific Views

If you need to disable CSRF protection for a particular view, you can use the `@csrf_exempt` decorator:

python

```python
from django.views.decorators.csrf import csrf_exempt
```

195

```
@csrf_exempt
def my_view(request):
    # The CSRF protection is skipped for this
view
    return    HttpResponse('CSRF    protection
disabled')
```

16.2.3 Clickjacking Protection

Clickjacking is an attack where a user is tricked into clicking something different from what they perceive, potentially leading to unwanted actions on a different site. Django provides **Clickjacking protection** via the X-Frame-Options HTTP header.

Enabling Clickjacking Protection in Django

By default, Django includes the X-Frame-Options middleware, which prevents the application from being embedded in an iframe unless explicitly allowed.

To enable or customize Clickjacking protection, add the following to your settings.py:

```
python
```

```
X_FRAME_OPTIONS = 'DENY'  # Prevents the site
from being embedded in any frame
# Or
X_FRAME_OPTIONS = 'SAMEORIGIN'  # Allows the site
to be embedded in frames on the same domain
```

16.3 Security Settings and Performance Optimizations

16.3.1 General Security Best Practices in Django

Django has a number of **security settings** that help you protect your application from various attacks.

1. HTTPS:

Ensure that your site is served over **HTTPS** by setting SECURE_SSL_REDIRECT to True:

```python
```

```
SECURE_SSL_REDIRECT = True
```

2. Secure Cookies:

Ensure that cookies are transmitted over secure channels and are not accessible via JavaScript by enabling the following settings:

```
python
```

```
SESSION_COOKIE_SECURE = True
CSRF_COOKIE_SECURE = True
```

3. HTTP Strict Transport Security (HSTS):

Enable HTTP Strict Transport Security (HSTS) to instruct browsers to only connect to your site over HTTPS:

```
python
```

```
SECURE_HSTS_SECONDS = 3600   # The duration for
which browsers should only access the site via
HTTPS
SECURE_HSTS_INCLUDE_SUBDOMAINS   =   True      #
Optional: Apply HSTS to all subdomains
```

4. Content Security Policy (CSP):

Content Security Policy (CSP) helps prevent XSS and data injection attacks by defining which resources can be loaded by the browser. You can configure CSP using middleware or through the HTTP headers.

16.3.2 Performance Optimizations for Django

To ensure that your Django app performs optimally in production, follow these best practices:

1. Enable Gzip Compression:

Compressing response content can improve load times and reduce bandwidth.

python

```python
MIDDLEWARE = [
    'django.middleware.gzip.GZipMiddleware',   # Add GzipMiddleware
]
```

2. Database Optimizations:

- **Use database indexes** to speed up queries.
- **Use database connection pooling** to reduce the overhead of establishing connections.

3. Caching:

Implement caching to speed up page load times and reduce the load on your database.

python

```python
CACHES = {
```

Go Programming Essentials

```
'default': {
    'BACKEND':
'django.core.cache.backends.memcached.Memcached
Cache',
    'LOCATION': '127.0.0.1:11211',
  }
}
```

4. Use Django's `select_related` *and* `prefetch_related:`

When querying related models, use `select_related` (for **ForeignKey** and **OneToOneField** relationships) and `prefetch_related` (for **ManyToManyField** and reverse relationships) to optimize database queries.

```python
python

# Use select_related for ForeignKey and OneToOne
relationships
queryset                              =
MyModel.objects.select_related('related_model')
.all()

# Use prefetch_related for ManyToMany and reverse
relationships
queryset                              =
MyModel.objects.prefetch_related('related_set')
.all()
```

16.4 Summary

Concept	Description
Django Middleware	A framework to process requests and responses globally.
CSRF Protection	Prevents cross-site request forgery attacks using tokens.
Clickjacking Protection	Prevents embedding the site in an iframe using the X-Frame-Options header.
Security Best Practices	HTTPS, secure cookies, HSTS, CSP, and other settings.
Performance Optimizations	Gzip compression, caching, database optimization, and query optimizations.

Next Chapter: Scaling Django Applications for Production

In the next chapter, we will:

- **Scale Django applications** to handle high traffic.
- **Set up load balancing** and **database replication**.

- **Deploy Django applications** to cloud platforms like AWS and GCP.

CHAPTER 17

DEPLOYING DJANGO APPLICATIONS

Deploying your Django application to the cloud is a key part of the development lifecycle. In this chapter, we will cover:

- **Hosting Django apps on DigitalOcean, AWS, and Heroku**
- **Setting up production environments**
- **Using Docker and CI/CD for Django projects**

17.1 Hosting Django Apps on DigitalOcean, AWS, and Heroku

17.1.1 Hosting on DigitalOcean

DigitalOcean is a simple cloud platform that offers **virtual private servers** (called Droplets) to host your Django applications.

Steps to Host Django on DigitalOcean:

1. **Create a Droplet**:
   Sign in to DigitalOcean and create a **Droplet** (a Linux-based virtual machine). Choose the latest **Ubuntu** image for simplicity.

2. **Connect to the Droplet**:
   Once the Droplet is created, connect to it using SSH:

   sh

   ```sh
   ssh root@your_droplet_ip
   ```

3. **Install Dependencies**:
   o Update and upgrade the server:

   sh

   ```sh
   sudo apt update && sudo apt upgrade
   ```

   o Install **Python, pip, and virtualenv**:

   sh

   ```sh
   sudo apt install python3 python3-pip python3-venv
   ```

- o Install **PostgreSQL** (or your preferred database):

sh

```
sudo    apt    install    postgresql
postgresql-contrib
```

4. **Set Up Your Django Project**:
   - o Clone your Django project repository or the code to the server.
   - o Set up a **virtual environment** and install dependencies:

sh

```
python3 -m venv myenv
source myenv/bin/activate
pip install -r requirements.txt
```

5. **Configure Gunicorn and Nginx**: Use **Gunicorn** as the WSGI server and **Nginx** as a reverse proxy for production:
   - o Install **Gunicorn**:

sh

```
pip install gunicorn
```

205

- o Create a **systemd service** for Gunicorn to manage your application.
- o Set up **Nginx** to forward requests to Gunicorn.

6. **Set Up the Database**:
   - o Create a database in PostgreSQL and connect it to your Django project in `settings.py`.
   - o Run migrations:

   ```sh
   python manage.py migrate
   ```

7. **Set Up Static and Media Files**:
   - o Collect static files:

   ```sh
   python manage.py collectstatic
   ```

8. **Secure the Server**:
   - o Configure **firewall rules** to allow traffic on HTTP (80) and HTTPS (443).
   - o Set up **SSL certificates** (using **Let's Encrypt** for free SSL certificates).

9. **Start the Django Application**:

o Restart the **Gunicorn** service to make the app live.

17.1.2 Hosting on AWS

AWS provides a powerful set of services for hosting applications, including EC2 (Elastic Compute Cloud), RDS (Relational Database Service), and S3 (Simple Storage Service).

Steps to Host Django on AWS EC2:

1. **Create an EC2 Instance**:
   o Sign in to AWS and create an EC2 instance with an Ubuntu or Amazon Linux AMI.
   o Choose an appropriate instance size and configure security groups to allow HTTP, HTTPS, and SSH.

2. **Connect to the EC2 Instance**:
   o Connect via SSH:

   ```sh
   ssh -i your-key.pem ubuntu@your_ec2_ip
   ```

3. **Install** **Dependencies**: Similar to DigitalOcean, install **Python, pip, Gunicorn, Nginx,** and **PostgreSQL** (or your database of choice).

4. **Set Up Your Django Application**:
   - your Django project to the instance.
   - Set up a **virtual environment**, install dependencies, and configure your **production settings** (like database, allowed hosts, etc.).

5. **Configure** **Gunicorn** **and** **Nginx**: Set up **Gunicorn** as the WSGI server and **Nginx** as the reverse proxy, similar to DigitalOcean steps.

6. **Deploy** **the** **App**: Run migrations, collect static files, and start the application.

17.1.3 Hosting on Heroku

Heroku is a **Platform-as-a-Service (PaaS)** that simplifies app deployment.

Steps to Host Django on Heroku:

1. **Create a Heroku Account**: Sign up for a free Heroku account at https://www.heroku.com.

2. **Install the Heroku CLI**: Follow the instructions to install the **Heroku Command Line Interface (CLI)**.

3. **Prepare Your Django App for Heroku**:
   o Ensure you have a `Procfile` in the root of your project to specify how to run the app:

   ```makefile
   web: gunicorn myproject.wsgi
   ```

   o Add **Heroku's Postgres database** to your app:

   ```sh
   heroku addons:create heroku-postgresql:hobby-dev
   ```

   o Configure your **ALLOWED_HOSTS** and **DATABASES** settings in `settings.py`.

4. **Deploy the Application**:

o   Login to Heroku:

```sh
heroku login
```

o   Create a new Heroku app:

```sh
heroku create my-django-app
```

o   Deploy via Git:

```sh
git push heroku master
```

5. **Set Up Static and Media Files**: Use **Heroku's S3 add-on** for static file hosting or **Django's `django-storage`** library to use S3 as the storage backend.

6. **Scale the Application**:

o   Scale your app's web dynos:

```sh
heroku ps:scale web=1
```

7. **Visit the App**: Once deployed, you can access your app at the Heroku-generated URL.

17.2 Setting Up Production Environments

17.2.1 Using Django Settings for Production

Configure `settings.py` for production by setting the following:

- **Database Configuration**: Use environment variables or **Django-environ** to securely store database credentials.
- **Allowed Hosts**: Limit access to your application:

  python

  ```
  ALLOWED_HOSTS = ['yourdomain.com']
  ```

- **Static and Media Files**: Use cloud storage like AWS S3 for storing static and media files in production.
- **Logging**: Set up logging for debugging in production:

```python
LOGGING = {
    'version': 1,
    'disable_existing_loggers': False,
    'handlers': {
        'file': {
            'level': 'ERROR',
            'class':
'logging.FileHandler',
            'filename': 'error.log',
        },
    },
    'loggers': {
        'django': {
            'handlers': ['file'],
            'level': 'ERROR',
            'propagate': True,
        },
    },
}
```

17.2.2 Performance Considerations

- **Caching**: Use **Memcached** or **Redis** for caching database queries, sessions, and templates.
- **Database Optimization**: Use **indexes** and **database migrations** for optimizing queries.

- **Load Balancing**: Distribute incoming traffic across multiple instances of your app.
- **Content Delivery Network (CDN)**: Use a CDN (e.g., AWS CloudFront) to serve static files faster globally.

17.3 Using Docker and CI/CD for Django Projects

17.3.1 Dockerizing Django Projects

To containerize your Django app using **Docker**, follow these steps:

1. **Create a Dockerfile** (similar to what we covered earlier).
2. **Build the Docker image**:

```sh
docker build -t my-django-app .
```

3. **Run the Docker container**:

```sh
docker run -p 8000:8000 my-django-app
```

4. **Push the image to Docker Hub**:

213

```sh
sh
```

```sh
docker push my-django-app
```

17.3.2 Setting Up CI/CD with GitHub Actions

To automate deployment using **GitHub Actions**:

1. Create a `.github/workflows/deploy.yml` file in your repository.
2. Set up continuous deployment for **Heroku** or **AWS**.

Example GitHub Actions configuration for deploying to Heroku:

```yaml
yaml

name: Deploy Django App

on:
  push:
    branches:
      - master

jobs:
  deploy:
    runs-on: ubuntu-latest
    steps:
```

```
- name: Checkout code
  uses: actions/checkout@v2

- name: Set up Python
  uses: actions/setup-python@v2
  with:
    python-version: '3.x'

- name: Install dependencies
  run: |
    pip install -r requirements.txt
    sudo apt-get install python3-dev

- name: Deploy to Heroku
  env:
    HEROKU_API_KEY:                    ${{
secrets.HEROKU_API_KEY }}
    run: |
      heroku login --api-key $HEROKU_API_KEY
      git        remote        add        heroku
https://git.heroku.com/your-app.git
      git push heroku master
```

17.4 Summary

Concept	Description
Hosting on DigitalOcean, AWS, Heroku	Steps for deploying Django apps to cloud platforms.
Setting Up Production Environments	Configure `settings.py`, database, and static files for production.
Dockerizing Django	Create Docker images for consistent deployment.
CI/CD with GitHub Actions	Automate deployment workflows with GitHub Actions.

Next Chapter: Monitoring and Debugging Django Applications in Production

In the next chapter, we will:

- Set up **monitoring and logging** for Django apps.
- Implement **error tracking** using tools like Sentry.
- Optimize Django apps in production for **high availability**.

CHAPTER 18

DISTRIBUTED SYSTEMS AND EVENT-DRIVEN ARCHITECTURES

Distributed systems enable applications to scale, handle failures gracefully, and provide high availability. These systems are essential for modern cloud-based applications, especially when working with **microservices** and **event-driven architectures**. In this chapter, we will cover:

- **Basics of distributed systems**
- **Implementing event-driven communication**
- **Real-world example: A microservices-based e-commerce platform**

18.1 Basics of Distributed Systems

18.1.1 What is a Distributed System?

A **distributed system** is a system in which components located on different networked computers communicate and coordinate to achieve a common goal. These systems are designed to:

- **Scale**: Handle growing loads by distributing the workload across multiple nodes.
- **Fault tolerance**: Continue operating even if some components fail.
- **Concurrency**: Handle multiple tasks simultaneously across distributed nodes.

18.1.2 Key Characteristics of Distributed Systems

1. **Scalability**: The ability to scale horizontally by adding more nodes.
2. **Fault tolerance**: The system remains operational even when parts of it fail.
3. **Consistency**: Ensures that all nodes in the system reflect the same state (often through mechanisms like **CAP Theorem**).
4. **Latency**: Communication between nodes may incur delay, especially in large systems.
5. **Distributed State**: Data and state are spread across multiple machines and locations.

18.1.3 Types of Distributed Systems

Type	Description
Client-Server	A client requests services, and the server provides them.
Peer-to-Peer (P2P)	Each node acts both as a client and a server.
Microservices	An architecture where each service runs independently, communicating via APIs.
Event-Driven	Components communicate via events, often using message brokers.

18.1.4 Challenges in Distributed Systems

1. **Network Partitioning**: Network failures may isolate parts of the system.
2. **Consistency vs. Availability**: Ensuring data consistency across nodes while maintaining availability (based on the **CAP Theorem**).
3. **Coordination**: Ensuring that all nodes are synchronized and handle tasks efficiently.
4. **Latency**: The time taken for messages to travel between distributed components.

18.2 Implementing Event-Driven Communication

Event-driven architecture (EDA) is a system design that uses events to trigger and communicate between services. It is especially useful in **distributed systems** for decoupling services and improving scalability.

18.2.1 What is Event-Driven Architecture?

Event-driven architecture is based on the production, detection, and consumption of **events**. An event is a **state change** that one component emits and other components react to.

Components of Event-Driven Architecture:

- **Event producers**: These services or components emit events when state changes occur (e.g., a user places an order).
- **Event consumers**: Other services that listen for events and act upon them (e.g., the shipping service starts processing after receiving an order event).
- **Event brokers**: Centralized systems like **Kafka, RabbitMQ**, or **AWS SQS** that distribute events to consumers.

18.2.2 How Event-Driven Communication Works

1. **Event Production**: An event is created by a service (e.g., when a new order is placed on the e-commerce site).
2. **Event Messaging**: The event is sent to a message broker like **Kafka** or **RabbitMQ**.
3. **Event Consumption**: Another service (e.g., payment processing service) consumes the event and processes it.
4. **Event Acknowledgment**: After processing, the consumer acknowledges receipt of the event.

Example of Event-Driven System

Imagine an **e-commerce platform** where several services need to react to specific events like order creation, payment, and shipment:

1. **Order Service** emits an event when a user places an order.
2. **Payment Service** consumes the order event, processes the payment, and emits a payment successful event.
3. **Shipping Service** listens for the payment successful event and processes the shipment.

18.2.3 Choosing the Right Message Broker

Broker	Use Case	Pros	Cons
Kafka	High-throughput messaging, stream processing.	Highly scalable, fault-tolerant	Setup and management complexity
RabbitMQ	Asynchronous communication for lightweight messages.	Easy to configure and use	Less suitable for high-throughput scenarios
AWS SQS	Managed queue service for decoupling microservices.	Fully managed by AWS, scalable	Limited features compared to Kafka
Redis Streams	Lightweight event processing and message queueing.	Fast and easy to use	Limited durability compared to others

18.3 Real-World Example: A Microservices-Based E-Commerce Platform

Let's consider a microservices-based **e-commerce platform** that handles various components like **orders, payments**, and **shipping**. Each service is **independent** and communicates asynchronously using events.

18.3.1 System Architecture

1. **Order Service**: Manages customer orders and emits an event (`OrderPlaced`) when a new order is placed.
2. **Payment Service**: Listens for `OrderPlaced` events, processes payments, and emits a `PaymentProcessed` event.
3. **Shipping Service**: Listens for the `PaymentProcessed` event and ships the product once payment is confirmed.

High-Level Workflow:

1. A customer places an order.
2. The **Order Service** emits an `OrderPlaced` event.
3. The **Payment Service** listens for the `OrderPlaced` event, processes the payment, and emits a `PaymentProcessed` event.

4. The **Shipping** **Service** listens for the PaymentProcessed event and prepares the order for shipment.

18.3.2 Implementing the E-Commerce Platform with Go

Let's briefly outline the services and their event-driven communication:

Order Service (Producer of Events):
go

```
package main

import (
    "fmt"
    "github.com/streadway/amqp"
)

func publishOrderEvent(orderDetails string) error {
    conn, err := amqp.Dial("amqp://guest:guest@localhost:5672/")
    if err != nil {
        return err
```

```go
    }
    defer conn.Close()

    ch, err := conn.Channel()
    if err != nil {
        return err
    }
    defer ch.Close()

    q, err := ch.QueueDeclare("orderQueue",
false, false, false, false, nil)
    if err != nil {
        return err
    }

    body := "OrderPlaced: " + orderDetails
    err = ch.Publish("", q.Name, false, false,
amqp.Publishing{
        ContentType: "text/plain",
        Body:        []byte(body),
    })
    if err != nil {
        return err
    }
    fmt.Println("OrderPlaced event published!")
    return nil
}

func main() {
```

```go
    orderDetails := "Order ID: 12345, Item:
Laptop"
    err := publishOrderEvent(orderDetails)
    if err != nil {
        fmt.Println("Error:", err)
    }
}
```

Payment Service (Consumer of Events):

```go
go

package main

import (
    "fmt"
    "github.com/streadway/amqp"
)

func consumeOrderEvent() {
    conn,              err              :=
amqp.Dial("amqp://guest:guest@localhost:5672/")
    if err != nil {
        fmt.Println("Error:", err)
        return
    }
    defer conn.Close()

    ch, err := conn.Channel()
    if err != nil {
        fmt.Println("Error:", err)
```

```go
        return
    }
    defer ch.Close()

    q, err := ch.QueueDeclare("orderQueue",
false, false, false, false, nil)
    if err != nil {
        fmt.Println("Error:", err)
        return
    }

    msgs, err := ch.Consume(q.Name, "", true,
false, false, false, nil)
    if err != nil {
        fmt.Println("Error:", err)
        return
    }

    for msg := range msgs {
        fmt.Println("Received   order   event:",
string(msg.Body))
        // Simulate payment processing
        fmt.Println("Processing payment...")
        // Emit PaymentProcessed event
    }
}

func main() {
    consumeOrderEvent()
```

}

18.3.3 Scaling the Platform with Kubernetes

- **Deploy the microservices** as separate **Kubernetes pods** to allow independent scaling.
- Use **Kafka** or **RabbitMQ** as the event broker to ensure smooth communication.
- Scale the services horizontally based on demand (e.g., scaling the Payment Service during sales).

18.4 Summary

Concept	Description
Distributed Systems	Systems where components are spread across multiple nodes, working together to handle requests.
Event-Driven Architecture	Asynchronous communication between services through events, improving scalability and resilience.
Microservices in E-Commerce	Independent services communicating via events, enabling a scalable and resilient architecture.

Concept	Description
Message Brokers	Tools like **RabbitMQ**, **Kafka**, and **AWS SQS** for event-driven communication.

Next Chapter: Monitoring Distributed Systems

In the next chapter, we will:

- Set up **monitoring** and **logging** for distributed systems.
- Implement **distributed tracing** to track requests across services.
- Optimize performance in **high-traffic distributed applications**.

CHAPTER 19

API GATEWAY AND SERVICE DISCOVERY

In distributed systems and microservices architectures, two critical components are the **API Gateway** and **Service Discovery**. These components help manage communication between microservices and ensure that services are discoverable in dynamic environments. In this chapter, we will explore:

- **What is an API Gateway?**
- **Using Kong or Nginx with Go microservices**
- **Service discovery with Consul**

19.1 What is an API Gateway?

19.1.1 Definition of an API Gateway

An **API Gateway** is a server that acts as an **entry point** into a system, typically in a microservices architecture. It acts as a **reverse proxy** that handles requests from clients and routes them to the appropriate microservice. The API Gateway can also perform additional functions such as:

- **Routing requests** to the correct service based on the URL or HTTP method.
- **Load balancing** requests across multiple instances of a service.
- **Authentication and Authorization** by validating tokens or user credentials.
- **Rate limiting and request throttling** to prevent abuse of the API.
- **Logging and Monitoring** for tracking API usage and performance.
- **Response transformation** to modify responses before they reach the client.

19.1.2 Why Use an API Gateway?

- **Simplification of client communication**: Clients communicate with a single entry point rather than multiple services.
- **Centralized management**: API Gateway centralizes security, monitoring, and logging, making it easier to manage cross-cutting concerns.
- **Decoupling of services**: The API Gateway can abstract service details from clients, making it easier to evolve backend services.

19.2 Using Kong or Nginx with Go Microservices

Both **Kong** and **Nginx** are popular choices for implementing an API Gateway in a microservices architecture.

19.2.1 Using Kong with Go Microservices

Kong is an open-source **API Gateway** and microservices management layer. It provides a range of features such as API routing, authentication, rate limiting, and monitoring.

Steps to Set Up Kong with Go Microservices:

1. **Install   Kong**:
   Install Kong on your local machine or use Docker to set up Kong as a containerized service:

   sh

   ```
   docker run -d --name kong \
       -e "KONG_DATABASE=off" \
       -e
   "KONG_DECLARATIVE_CONFIG=/kong/kong.yml" \
       -e
   "KONG_PORT_MAPS=8000:8000,8001:8001" \
       -p 8000:8000 -p 8001:8001 \
       kong:latest
   ```

2. **Set up your Go microservices**: Let's assume you have multiple Go microservices running, such as an **Order Service** and a **Payment Service**.

3. **Configure Kong to Route Requests to Go Microservices**:

   In Kong, define routes to map incoming requests to the respective Go services.

   Example Kong configuration (`kong.yml`):

   yaml

```yaml
services:
  - name: order-service
    url: http://localhost:8081
    routes:
      - name: order-route
        paths:
          - /orders
  - name: payment-service
    url: http://localhost:8082
    routes:
      - name: payment-route
        paths:
          - /payments
```

4. **Access the services**:
Once Kong is running, you can send API requests to Kong, which will route them to the correct microservice:

sh

```
curl http://localhost:8000/orders
curl http://localhost:8000/payments
```

5. **Add Features to Kong**:
Kong allows you to enable features like **Authentication, Rate Limiting**, and **Logging** via plugins.

Example: Enabling **JWT authentication** for the order-service:

sh

```
curl        -i        -X        PATCH
http://localhost:8001/services/order-
service/plugins \
    --data "name=jwt"
```

19.2.2 Using Nginx with Go Microservices

Nginx is a high-performance web server and reverse proxy server that can also act as an API Gateway.

Steps to Set Up Nginx with Go Microservices:

1. **Install   Nginx**:
   You can install Nginx using the package manager or use Docker for easier setup:

   ```sh
   docker run --name nginx -d -p 80:80 nginx
   ```

2. **Configure Nginx to Proxy Requests**:
   Nginx configuration can be set up to forward requests to your Go services. Add the following configuration to your `nginx.conf`:

   ```nginx
   http {
       upstream order-service {
           server localhost:8081;
       }

       upstream payment-service {
           server localhost:8082;
       }
   ```

```
server {
    listen 80;

    location /orders {
        proxy_pass        http://order-
service;
    }

    location /payments {
        proxy_pass        http://payment-
service;
    }
}
}
```

3. **Restart** **Nginx**:

After configuring Nginx, restart it to apply the changes:

```sh
sh
```

```
docker restart nginx
```

4. **Access** **the** **Services**:

Now, you can access your Go services through the Nginx gateway:

```sh
sh
```

```
curl http://localhost/orders
curl http://localhost/payments
```

19.3 Service Discovery with Consul

Service discovery is a critical aspect of microservices, especially in dynamic environments where services can be added or removed frequently. **Consul** is a popular tool for managing service discovery and configuration.

19.3.1 What is Consul?

Consul is an open-source tool that provides:

- **Service Discovery**: Allows services to find and communicate with each other.
- **Health Checking**: Monitors the health of services and ensures requests are routed only to healthy instances.
- **Key-Value Store**: Stores configuration data that can be accessed by services.

19.3.2 Setting Up Consul for Service Discovery

Step 1: Install Consul

You can install Consul locally or use Docker for simplicity:

```sh
sh
```

```sh
docker     run     -d     --name=consul     -e
CONSUL_LOCAL_CONFIG='{"skip_leave_on_interrupt"
: true}' -p 8500:8500 consul
```

Step 2: Register Services with Consul

Your Go microservices need to register themselves with Consul so that they can be discovered by other services.

Example: Register the **Order Service** with Consul:

```go
go

package main

import (
    "github.com/hashicorp/consul/api"
    "log"
)

func main() {
    client,                 err                 :=
api.NewClient(api.DefaultConfig())
    if err != nil {
```

```
        log.Fatal(err)
    }

    registration                          :=
&api.AgentServiceRegistration{
        ID:       "order-service",
        Name:     "order-service",
        Address:  "localhost",
        Port:     8081,
    }

    err                                    =
client.Agent().ServiceRegister(registration)
    if err != nil {
        log.Fatal(err)
    }

    log.Println("Service      registered      with
Consul!")
}
```

Step 3: Discover Services with Consul

To discover the **Order Service**, you can query the Consul
API:

```sh
sh
```

```
curl
http://localhost:8500/v1/catalog/service/order-
service
```

The response will contain the details of the `order-service` instance, including the address and port, which can be used by other services to make requests.

19.3.3 Integrating Consul with Go Microservices

- **Service Registration**: Each service (e.g., `order-service`, `payment-service`) registers itself with Consul when it starts.
- **Service Discovery**: When a service needs to communicate with another (e.g., the `payment-service` needs to access the `order-service`), it queries Consul for the location of the `order-service`.

This decouples services and allows them to **dynamically discover each other** without hardcoding addresses or IPs.

19.4 Summary

Concept	Description
API Gateway	Centralized entry point for microservices, routing and managing requests.
Using Kong	Kong is an open-source API Gateway for managing microservices, with support for plugins like authentication and rate limiting.
Using Nginx	Nginx can be used as an API Gateway and reverse proxy for microservices.
Service Discovery	Service discovery with **Consul** allows microservices to dynamically find and communicate with each other.
Consul Integration	Consul registers services and enables service discovery, health checking, and configuration management.

Next Chapter: Advanced Topics in Microservices Architecture

In the next chapter, we will:

- **Explore advanced microservices patterns** like **CQRS, Event Sourcing**, and **Saga Pattern**.
- Implement **API versioning, load balancing**, and **resilience patterns** for microservices.

CHAPTER 20

SCALING MICROSERVICES WITH GO

Scaling microservices efficiently is crucial for handling increasing traffic and ensuring that applications remain responsive and reliable. This chapter focuses on:

- **Load balancing techniques**
- **Horizontal vs. vertical scaling**
- **Deploying Go microservices to Kubernetes**

20.1 Load Balancing Techniques

20.1.1 What is Load Balancing?

Load balancing distributes incoming network traffic across multiple servers or instances of a service to ensure that no single server is overwhelmed, improving both **availability** and **fault tolerance**. It helps in **scaling applications** to handle increased traffic and ensures that the load is balanced evenly across microservices or servers.

20.1.2 Types of Load Balancing

There are different types of load balancing techniques:

1. Round-Robin Load Balancing

This is the simplest form of load balancing, where requests are distributed evenly across all available servers.

Example:

- Request 1 → Server 1
- Request 2 → Server 2
- Request 3 → Server 3
- Request 4 → Server 1
- And so on...

2. Weighted Round-Robin

In this method, some servers receive more traffic than others based on predefined weights. Servers with higher weights receive more requests.

3. Least Connections

In this approach, the server with the **least active connections** is selected to handle the next incoming request. This is beneficial when servers have varying capabilities.

4. IP Hashing

Requests are directed to a specific server based on the client's IP address. This ensures that the same client is always routed to the same server.

20.1.3 Implementing Load Balancing in Go

In Go, load balancing can be handled using **Nginx** or a **reverse proxy** server. Alternatively, cloud providers such as AWS, GCP, and Azure offer managed load balancing solutions.

Example: Implementing Load Balancing with Nginx

1. **Nginx Configuration**: In Nginx, you can configure load balancing with multiple backend services using the `upstream` directive.

Example `nginx.conf`:

```
nginx

http {
    upstream go_microservices {
        server go-service-1:8080;
        server go-service-2:8080;
        server go-service-3:8080;
    }

    server {
        listen 80;

        location / {
            proxy_pass
http://go_microservices;
            proxy_set_header Host $host;
            proxy_set_header     X-Real-IP
$remote_addr;
            proxy_set_header X-Forwarded-
For $proxy_add_x_forwarded_for;
            proxy_set_header X-Forwarded-
Proto $scheme;
        }
    }
}
```

2. **Running Nginx**:

o Start Nginx with the above configuration.

o Nginx will distribute incoming requests to the available **Go microservices** (server 1, server 2, or server 3).

20.2 Horizontal vs. Vertical Scaling

20.2.1 What is Scaling?

Scaling refers to the ability to handle growing traffic by adding resources. There are two primary approaches to scaling:

1. Horizontal Scaling (Scaling Out)

Horizontal scaling involves adding **more instances** of your microservices to distribute the load. It is the most common method of scaling microservices, especially in cloud environments.

- **Pros**:
    o Easily handles increasing load.
    o Provides better fault tolerance (if one instance fails, others are still available).
    o Commonly used in cloud-based applications.
- **Cons**:

- o Requires a **load balancer** to distribute traffic evenly across instances.
- o Can lead to challenges in managing state across multiple instances.

2. Vertical Scaling (Scaling Up)

Vertical scaling involves upgrading the resources (CPU, memory, storage) of a single instance to handle more traffic. This type of scaling is usually limited by the hardware of the server.

- **Pros**:
    - o Simpler to implement (you don't need a load balancer).
    - o Suitable for applications with high memory or CPU usage.
- **Cons**:
    - o Limited by the physical capabilities of the server.
    - o If a server fails, the entire application may be impacted.

When to Use Horizontal vs. Vertical Scaling?

- Use **horizontal scaling** when you want to scale a microservice across multiple nodes, ensuring high availability and handling growing traffic.

- Use **vertical scaling** for legacy systems or when you can't scale horizontally due to limitations in the application architecture.

20.3 Deploying Go Microservices to Kubernetes

Kubernetes is a powerful platform for **automating deployment, scaling**, and **management** of containerized applications, including **Go microservices**.

20.3.1 What is Kubernetes?

Kubernetes (K8s) is an open-source system for automating the deployment, scaling, and management of containerized applications. It supports **horizontal scaling, self-healing**, and **service discovery**, making it ideal for running **Go microservices** in production environments.

20.3.2 Setting Up Go Microservices with Kubernetes

1. **Create Docker Images for Your Go Microservices**:

- o Dockerize your Go application using the Dockerfile we discussed earlier.
- o Build and push the Docker image to a container registry like **Docker Hub**, **AWS ECR**, or **Google Container Registry**.

Example Dockerfile:

```
dockerfile

FROM golang:1.20 AS builder
WORKDIR /app
 . .

RUN go build -o app .

FROM alpine:latest
 --from=builder /app/app /app
EXPOSE 8080
CMD ["/app"]
```

2. **Create Kubernetes Deployment YAML**: Deploy your Go microservices as pods in Kubernetes. You can define the deployment in a YAML file that describes the number of replicas, the Docker image, and environment variables.

Example `go-microservice-deployment.yaml`:

250

```yaml
yaml

apiVersion: apps/v1
kind: Deployment
metadata:
  name: go-microservice
spec:
  replicas: 3
  selector:
    matchLabels:
      app: go-microservice
  template:
    metadata:
      labels:
        app: go-microservice
    spec:
      containers:
        - name: go-microservice
          image: your-docker-image
          ports:
            - containerPort: 8080
```

3. **Create Kubernetes Service YAML**: Expose your Go microservice using a Kubernetes service. This allows other services to discover and communicate with your Go service.

Example go-microservice-service.yaml:

```yaml
apiVersion: v1
kind: Service
metadata:
  name: go-microservice
spec:
  selector:
    app: go-microservice
  ports:
    - protocol: TCP
      port: 80
      targetPort: 8080
  type: LoadBalancer
```

4. **Apply the Kubernetes Configurations**: Once your YAML files are ready, apply them to your Kubernetes cluster using `kubectl`:

```sh
kubectl apply -f go-microservice-deployment.yaml
kubectl apply -f go-microservice-service.yaml
```

5. **Verify the Deployment**: Check if the deployment and service are running correctly:

```sh
```

```
kubectl get deployments
kubectl get pods
kubectl get services
```

If you are using a cloud provider with **LoadBalancer** type services, Kubernetes will provision an external IP to access your microservice.

20.3.3 Auto-Scaling in Kubernetes

Kubernetes provides **Horizontal Pod Autoscaling (HPA),** which automatically scales the number of pods in a deployment based on observed CPU or memory utilization.

To enable **HPA** for your Go microservice:

1. **Install Metrics Server** (if not already installed):

```sh
```

```
kubectl            apply            -f
https://github.com/kubernetes-
sigs/metrics-
```

```
server/releases/latest/download/component
s.yaml
```

2. Create an HPA resource:

```yaml
apiVersion: autoscaling/v2beta2
kind: HorizontalPodAutoscaler
metadata:
  name: go-microservice-hpa
spec:
  scaleTargetRef:
    apiVersion: apps/v1
    kind: Deployment
    name: go-microservice
  minReplicas: 2
  maxReplicas: 10
  metrics:
    - type: Resource
      resource:
        name: cpu
        target:
          type: Utilization
          averageUtilization: 50
```

3. Apply HPA:

```sh
```

```
kubectl apply -f go-microservice-hpa.yaml
```

This configuration will scale the number of pods for your Go microservice based on **CPU utilization**.

20.4 Summary

Concept		Description
Load Balancing		Techniques for distributing traffic across multiple instances of a service to ensure high availability and scalability.
Horizontal **Vertical Scaling**	**vs.**	Horizontal scaling adds more instances, while vertical scaling increases resource capacity of existing instances.
Deploying **Microservices** **Kubernetes**	**Go** **to**	Kubernetes allows you to automate the deployment, scaling, and management of containerized Go applications.
Auto-Scaling		Kubernetes supports Horizontal Pod Autoscaling (HPA) to automatically scale microservices based on resource usage.

Next Chapter: Monitoring and Logging in Microservices
Architecture

In the next chapter, we will:

- Set up **monitoring** for microservices using **Prometheus**
  and **Grafana**.
- Implement **distributed tracing** using tools like **Jaeger** or
  OpenTelemetry.
- Explore best practices for **logging** and **alerting** in
  microservices.

CHAPTER 21

PERFORMANCE OPTIMIZATION IN GO

As you develop more complex Go applications, performance becomes increasingly important. In this chapter, we will explore techniques and tools for optimizing the performance of your Go applications, including:

- **Benchmarking Go applications**
- **Profiling with `pprof`**
- **Optimizing memory usage**

21.1 Benchmarking Go Applications

21.1.1 Why Benchmarking is Important

Benchmarking allows you to measure the **performance** of specific parts of your application, ensuring that optimizations have the desired effect. In Go, benchmarking helps to compare different implementations, track performance regressions, and find bottlenecks.

Go provides built-in support for benchmarking via the **testing** package, which includes tools for creating benchmarks.

21.1.2 Writing Benchmarks in Go

Go's **testing package** provides a `testing.B` type for writing benchmarks. Benchmarks are defined using the `b` `*testing.B` parameter, and Go will run the benchmark function multiple times to get an accurate measure of the performance.

Example: Simple Benchmarking

Here's an example of a basic benchmarking function:

```go
package main

import (
    "testing"
)

// Function to benchmark
func sum(a, b int) int {
    return a + b
}
```

```
// Benchmark function
func BenchmarkSum(b *testing.B) {
    for i := 0; i < b.N; i++ {
        sum(1, 2)
    }
}
```

- **b.N**: The benchmark loop runs **b.N** times, and Go will automatically adjust **b.N** to ensure a statistically significant measurement.
- **testing.B**: The b variable allows you to measure the duration and adjust the number of iterations for your benchmark.

To run the benchmark:

sh

```
go test -bench .
```

21.1.3 Analyzing Benchmark Results

Go will output the **benchmark results** in nanoseconds per operation:

sh

```
BenchmarkSum-8      1000000000      0.247 ns/op
```

259

This shows how long it takes for the `sum()` function to execute for one iteration.

21.1.4 Benchmarking More Complex Code

Benchmarking complex code is important for identifying bottlenecks and ensuring that optimizations actually improve performance.

Example: Benchmarking a Sorting Algorithm

go

```
package main

import (
    "sort"
    "testing"
)

func BenchmarkSort(b *testing.B) {
    // Generate a large list of integers
    data := make([]int, 10000)
    for i := range data {
        data[i] = 10000 - i
    }
```

```
    b.ResetTimer()  // Reset the timer to exclude
setup time
    for i := 0; i < b.N; i++ {
        sort.Ints(data)
    }
}
```

21.1.5 Parallel Benchmarks

Go allows you to write **parallel benchmarks** to utilize multiple CPU cores. You can use b.RunParallel() to run benchmarks in parallel.

go

```
func BenchmarkSortParallel(b *testing.B) {
    b.RunParallel(func(pb *testing.PB) {
        for pb.Next() {
            sort.Ints(data)
        }
    })
}
```

21.2 Profiling with pprof

21.2.1 What is pprof?

pprof is a powerful profiling tool that helps you analyze and visualize the **performance** of your Go application. It provides insights into CPU usage, memory allocation, and goroutine blocking, which can help you identify performance bottlenecks.

Go's `net/http/pprof` package enables you to profile your application at runtime.

21.2.2 Setting Up pprof in Go

First, import the `net/http/pprof` package:

```go
import (
    _ "net/http/pprof"
    "net/http"
    "log"
)

func main() {
    // Start the pprof server
    go func() {

log.Println(http.ListenAndServe("localhost:6060
", nil))
    }()
```

```
    // Application logic...
}
```

The `net/http/pprof` package registers default routes for profiling (e.g., `/debug/pprof/heap`, `/debug/pprof/goroutine`, etc.).

- **`/debug/pprof/heap`**: Memory allocations (heap).
- **`/debug/pprof/goroutine`**: Goroutine stack traces.
- **`/debug/pprof/threadcreate`**: Thread creation.
- **`/debug/pprof/block`**: Goroutine blocking profile.

21.2.3 Profiling CPU Usage

To profile **CPU usage**, run your Go application with the pprof tool and pass the following URL:

sh

```
go          tool          pprof
http://localhost:6060/debug/pprof/profile?secon
ds=30
```

This will record 30 seconds of CPU profiling. After running the command, you can analyze the profile:

263

```sh
```

```
(pprof) top
```

The `top` command shows the functions that consume the most CPU.

21.2.4 Profiling Memory Usage

For memory profiling, use the heap profile:

```sh
```

```
go              tool              pprof
http://localhost:6060/debug/pprof/heap
```

You can view memory allocations with commands like `top` and `list` (for specific functions) to identify parts of the code that are allocating excessive memory.

21.3 Optimizing Memory Usage

21.3.1 Memory Allocation and Garbage Collection

Go has a **garbage collector** that automatically frees unused memory, but there are things you can do to optimize memory usage.

1. **Minimize Memory Allocations**: Avoid unnecessary memory allocations by reusing slices, arrays, and structs. This reduces the load on the garbage collector.

2. **Use Memory Pools**: Use **sync.Pool** for reusing objects, particularly when objects are expensive to allocate and deallocate.

```go
var bufferPool = sync.Pool{
    New: func() interface{} {
        return make([]byte, 0, 1024)
    },
}

func processData() {
    buf := bufferPool.Get().([]byte)
    defer bufferPool.Put(buf)
    // Use buf for processing
}
```

3. **Profile Memory Allocations**: Using **pprof** or the `testing` package, you can find areas of the code that allocate too much memory or create unnecessary objects.

4. **Avoid Memory Leaks**: Ensure that memory is properly deallocated after use and that objects are no longer referenced after they are no longer needed.

5. **Optimize Data Structures**: Choose efficient data structures for your problem. For example, use **maps** for fast lookups and **arrays/slices** for contiguous blocks of data.

21.3.2 Optimizing Goroutines

Goroutines can consume significant memory, especially when too many are created. Use goroutines efficiently by:

1. **Limiting the number of Goroutines**: Use a worker pool pattern to control the number of goroutines created.

2. **Avoiding Unnecessary Goroutines**: Ensure that goroutines are used for tasks that are truly concurrent. For tasks that don't need concurrency, use simple functions or avoid goroutines.

21.4 Summary

Concept	Description
Benchmarking in Go	Use the `testing` package to write benchmarks and measure performance in terms of time taken for execution.
pprof for Profiling	Use `pprof` to analyze CPU usage, memory allocations, and identify bottlenecks in Go applications.
Memory Optimization	Reduce memory allocations, use **sync.Pool**, and profile memory usage to optimize performance.

Next Chapter: Concurrency Patterns in Go

In the next chapter, we will explore advanced **concurrency patterns** in Go, including:

- **Worker Pools** and **fan-out/fan-in** models.
- **Pipeline patterns** and **rate limiting**.
- **Graceful shutdown** and handling errors in concurrent operations.

CHAPTER 22

WRITING HIGH-PERFORMANCE GO APPLICATIONS

Go is known for its **efficiency**, **concurrency**, and **scalability**, making it an ideal language for writing high-performance applications. In this chapter, we will cover:

- **Best practices for writing efficient Go code**
- **Real-world example: High-performance Go-based data processing pipeline**

22.1 Best Practices for Writing Efficient Go Code

Writing efficient Go code requires understanding both **Go-specific performance optimizations** and general **software engineering principles**. Let's explore several best practices to optimize the performance of your Go applications.

22.1.1 Efficient Memory Usage

1. **Avoid Unnecessary Memory Allocations**
   Excessive memory allocation can slow down your

application and trigger the **garbage collector** (GC) more often, resulting in performance degradation.

- o Reuse slices, arrays, and structs where possible.
- o Use **sync.Pool** to reuse objects that are expensive to allocate.

```go
var bufferPool = sync.Pool{
    New: func() interface{} {
        return make([]byte, 0, 1024)
    },
}

func processData() {
    buf := bufferPool.Get().([]byte)
    defer bufferPool.Put(buf) // Return buffer to pool
    // Use buf for processing
}
```

2. **Minimize   Object   Creation**
Create objects only when absolutely necessary. For example, avoid creating new slices or maps when you can reuse existing ones.

3. **Use   the   Right   Data   Structures**
Selecting the right data structure can have a significant impact on performance. For example:

- o Use **maps** for fast lookups.
- o Use **arrays** and **slices** for contiguous data storage.
- o Use **channels** efficiently to manage concurrency.

22.1.2 Effective Concurrency

Go's concurrency model, using **goroutines** and **channels**, is highly efficient, but it requires careful management to avoid issues such as goroutine leaks and excessive context switching.

1. **Limit**   **Goroutines**

   Too many concurrent goroutines can overwhelm the system. Use a **worker pool** pattern to limit the number of concurrently running goroutines.

```go
func worker(id int, jobs <-chan Job,
results chan<- Result) {
    for job := range jobs {
        result := processJob(job)  // Your
job processing logic
        results <- result
    }
```

```
}

func main() {
    jobs := make(chan Job, 100)
    results := make(chan Result, 100)
    for i := 0; i < 5; i++ {
        go worker(i, jobs, results)
    }
    // Send jobs and collect results
}
```

2. **Avoid Blocking Calls in Goroutines**
   Blocking calls (e.g., network I/O, database queries) can prevent your goroutines from being efficient. Offload blocking operations to worker pools or use **select statements** to handle multiple channels simultaneously.

22.1.3 Optimize I/O Operations

Efficient handling of **I/O** operations (disk, network, database) is crucial for performance. Here are a few tips to optimize I/O in Go:

1. **Use   Buffered   I/O**
   Buffered I/O helps minimize the number of system

271

calls by reading or writing larger chunks of data at once.

```go

buf := make([]byte, 4096)
n, err := file.Read(buf)
```

2. **Asynchronous   I/O**
   Use **goroutines** to handle I/O asynchronously, improving throughput by not blocking the main execution.

3. **Efficient   File   Handling**
   For file I/O, read and write data in large chunks, avoid small, frequent reads and writes that lead to inefficiency.

22.1.4 Profiling and Benchmarking

To write efficient Go code, you need to identify bottlenecks and optimize them.

1. **Benchmarking   with   testing.B**
   Benchmarking allows you to measure the performance of specific functions or code blocks.

```go
func BenchmarkSum(b *testing.B) {
    for i := 0; i < b.N; i++ {
        sum(1, 2)
    }
}
```

2. Profiling with pprof

Use **pprof** to profile CPU and memory usage of your application.

```go
import _ "net/http/pprof"
go func() {

log.Println(http.ListenAndServe("localhost:6060", nil))
}()
```

3. Optimize Hot · Paths

After profiling and benchmarking, focus on **hot paths**—the parts of the code where the most processing time is spent—and optimize them first.

22.1.5 Avoid Premature Optimizations

It's tempting to try to optimize your code early, but premature optimization can lead to **complexity** without significant benefits. The best approach is to:

1. **Measure performance** before optimization.
2. **Optimize the hot spots** that impact the most performance.

22.2 Real-World Example: High-Performance Go-Based Data Processing Pipeline

Now, let's walk through a **real-world example**: building a high-performance **data processing pipeline** in Go. This pipeline will process large volumes of data concurrently, efficiently, and in a fault-tolerant manner.

22.2.1 Design of the Data Processing Pipeline

We need to process a large dataset (e.g., logs, transaction records, etc.). The pipeline consists of multiple steps, including:

1. **Data ingestion**: Read data from an external source (e.g., a file or a stream).

2. **Data transformation**: Process the data (e.g., filtering, parsing).

3. **Data storage**: Store the processed data into a database or another service.

We'll use **goroutines** and **channels** to process data concurrently.

22.2.2 Implementing the Pipeline in Go

1. **Define the Data Structures and Workers**

```go

package main

import (
    "fmt"
    "sync"
)

type Data struct {
    ID      int
    Value string
}
```

```go
func transformData(data *Data) {
    // Example transformation: Append
"_processed" to the value
    data.Value += "_processed"
}


func storeData(data *Data, wg *sync.WaitGroup) {
    defer wg.Done()
    fmt.Printf("Storing Data: %d - %s\n",
data.ID, data.Value)
}


func worker(id int, dataChan <-chan Data, wg
*sync.WaitGroup) {
    for data := range dataChan {
        transformData(&data)  // Process the data
        storeData(&data, wg)     // Store the
processed data
    }
}


func main() {
    dataChan := make(chan Data, 100)
    var wg sync.WaitGroup

    // Start worker goroutines
    for i := 0; i < 5; i++ {
        go worker(i, dataChan, &wg)
```

```
    }

    // Simulate data ingestion
    for i := 1; i <= 10; i++ {
        dataChan    <-    Data{ID:    i,    Value:
fmt.Sprintf("Data %d", i)}
        wg.Add(1)
    }

    // Close the channel and wait for all
goroutines to finish
    close(dataChan)
    wg.Wait()
}
```

22.2.3 Explanation of the Code

- We define a `Data` struct to represent the data that will be processed.
- **`worker()`** is a function that processes data concurrently. It reads from the `dataChan` channel, transforms the data, and stores it.
- We start 5 goroutines to handle data concurrently.
- We simulate **data ingestion** by sending data into the `dataChan` channel.
- The **`sync.WaitGroup`** ensures that the main function waits for all goroutines to finish before exiting.

22.2.4 Running the Pipeline

Running the application will simulate processing data concurrently:

```sh
```

```sh
go run main.go
```

Output:

```sh
```

```sh
Storing Data: 1 - Data 1_processed
Storing Data: 2 - Data 2_processed
...
```

In this example, data is processed concurrently, and the workers run efficiently without blocking. This model is scalable, and more workers can be added to handle larger data volumes.

22.2.5 Optimizing the Pipeline

1. **Memory Efficiency**: Use **sync.Pool** to manage reusable objects, reducing memory allocations.

2. **Concurrency**: Tune the number of worker goroutines based on the available CPU resources (using **worker pools** or **goroutine pools**).

3. **Efficient Channels**: Use buffered channels to allow the workers to process data without waiting for the main function to consume it.

22.3 Summary

Concept	Description
Efficient Memory Usage	Minimize memory allocations, reuse objects, and use **sync.Pool** to optimize memory.
Effective Concurrency	Use goroutines efficiently, limit the number of goroutines, and use worker pools for parallel tasks.
Optimizing I/O	Use buffered I/O, asynchronous I/O, and optimize file handling to improve throughput.
Profiling and Benchmarking	Profile your code using **pprof**, and benchmark with the testing.B type for performance insights.

Concept	Description
Data Processing Pipeline	Build high-performance pipelines in Go using **goroutines**, **channels**, and **worker pools** for concurrency.

Next Chapter: Advanced Concurrency and Parallelism in Go

In the next chapter, we will explore advanced concurrency patterns in Go:

- **Parallelism vs. Concurrency**
- **Advanced synchronization patterns** such as **Mutex, RWMutex**, and **atomic operations**.
- **Managing high-concurrency workloads** with Go.

CHAPTER 23

TESTING AND CI/CD FOR GO APPLICATIONS

Testing and Continuous Integration/Continuous Deployment (CI/CD) are essential components of modern software development workflows. This chapter will guide you through:

- **Unit testing and integration testing in Go**
- **Setting up CI/CD pipelines for Go apps**
- **Automating deployments**

23.1 Unit Testing and Integration Testing in Go

23.1.1 Unit Testing in Go

Unit testing focuses on testing individual units of code, such as functions or methods, to ensure they work as expected. In Go, the **testing** package provides a powerful framework for writing and running tests.

Writing Unit Tests in Go

To create a unit test, you define a function that starts with `Test` and takes a `*testing.T` parameter. Here's an example:

```go
package main

import "testing"

// Function to test
func Add(a, b int) int {
    return a + b
}

// Unit test for the Add function
func TestAdd(t *testing.T) {
    result := Add(2, 3)
    expected := 5

    if result != expected {
        t.Errorf("Add(2, 3) = %d; want %d", result, expected)
    }
}
```

Running Unit Tests

To run your unit tests, use the `go test` command:

```sh
go test
```

This will execute all functions in your package that start with `Test`.

Test Coverage

Go also provides a way to check how much of your code is covered by tests:

```sh
go test -cover
```

23.1.2 Integration Testing in Go

Integration testing focuses on testing how different units or modules interact. These tests often involve external systems such as databases, APIs, or file systems.

Writing Integration Tests

For integration tests, you may need to set up external services (e.g., a database) and verify that your code interacts with them correctly.

Example of an integration test with a simple database:

```go
package main

import (
    "database/sql"
    "log"
    "testing"
    _ "github.com/lib/pq" // PostgreSQL driver
)

func TestDatabaseConnection(t *testing.T) {
    db, err := sql.Open("postgres", "user=test dbname=testdb sslmode=disable")
    if err != nil {
        t.Fatalf("Failed to connect to database: %v", err)
    }
    defer db.Close()

    // Check if the connection is alive
    if err := db.Ping(); err != nil {
        t.Fatalf("Failed to ping database: %v", err)
    }
}
```

In this example, we are testing whether we can establish a database connection and successfully interact with the database.

Mocking External Services

For tests that require external services (e.g., third-party APIs or external databases), it's common to **mock** those services. Libraries like `github.com/stretchr/testify/mock` or `github.com/golang/mock` allow you to create mock versions of interfaces to test your code without needing actual services.

23.2 Setting Up CI/CD Pipelines for Go Apps

23.2.1 What is CI/CD?

CI/CD (Continuous Integration and Continuous Deployment) is a set of practices to automatically build, test, and deploy code changes. It ensures that your application is always in a deployable state.

Steps in the CI/CD Process:

1. **Continuous Integration (CI)**: Automatically builds and tests your code every time a change is pushed to the repository.
2. **Continuous Deployment (CD)**: Automatically deploys the application after passing all tests.

23.2.2 Setting Up CI with GitHub Actions

GitHub Actions is a powerful tool to set up CI/CD workflows directly in GitHub repositories. Let's create a **GitHub Actions workflow** to run Go tests and build the application.

Creating a GitHub Actions Workflow File

1. **Create a `.github/workflows/ci.yml` file** in your GitHub repository:

```yaml
yaml


name: Go CI Workflow


on:
  push:
    branches:
      - main
```

```
  pull_request:
    branches:
      - main

jobs:
  build:
    runs-on: ubuntu-latest

    steps:
      - name: Checkout code
        uses: actions/checkout@v2

      - name: Set up Go
        uses: actions/setup-go@v2
        with:
          go-version: '1.17'

      - name: Install dependencies
        run: |
          go mod tidy

      - name: Run tests
        run: |
          go test -v ./...

      - name: Build the application
        run: |
          go build -o myapp .
```

Explanation of the Workflow:

- The workflow runs on every **push** to the `main` branch or on **pull requests** targeting `main`.
- The steps include:
  - **Checkout**: Checking out the code from the repository.
  - **Set up Go**: Setting up the Go environment with the specified version.
  - **Install dependencies**: Running `go mod tidy` to install any dependencies.
  - **Run tests**: Running `go test` to execute unit tests and validate the code.
  - **Build the application**: Building the application with `go build`.

To trigger the workflow, simply push a commit to your `main` branch or create a pull request.

Running the CI Pipeline

Once you push your changes to GitHub, GitHub Actions will automatically run the defined workflow. You can view the results in the **Actions** tab of your repository.

23.2.3 Setting Up CD with GitHub Actions

You can extend the CI workflow to deploy your application automatically after it passes the tests.

Here's how you can deploy to **Heroku** after a successful build:

```yaml
name: Go CD Workflow

on:
  push:
    branches:
      - main

jobs:
  build:
    runs-on: ubuntu-latest

    steps:
      - name: Checkout code
        uses: actions/checkout@v2

      - name: Set up Go
        uses: actions/setup-go@v2
        with:
          go-version: '1.17'
```

```
      - name: Install dependencies
        run: |
          go mod tidy


      - name: Run tests
        run: |
          go test -v ./...


      - name: Build the application
        run: |
          go build -o myapp .


      - name: Deploy to Heroku
        uses: akshnz/heroku-deploy@v1
        with:
          heroku_app_name:        'your-heroku-app-
name'
          heroku_email: 'your-heroku-email'
          heroku_api_key:                    ${{
secrets.HEROKU_API_KEY }}
```

Explanation:

- After building the Go app and running tests, the application is deployed to **Heroku** using the **Heroku deploy action**.
- The **Heroku API key** is stored securely in GitHub Secrets and is referenced using `${{ secrets.HEROKU_API_KEY }}`.

23.3.1 Why Automate Deployments?

Automating deployments reduces human errors and ensures that your application can be deployed easily, quickly, and consistently. It is essential for high-velocity development cycles and ensuring that your application is always up-to-date with the latest changes.

23.3.2 Example of Automating Deployment to Kubernetes

For deploying Go applications to **Kubernetes**, the CI/CD pipeline can include the following steps:

1. **Build the Docker Image**:
   o Create a `Dockerfile` and build your Go application into a containerized Docker image.
2. **Push the Image to Docker Hub or ECR**:
   o Push the built image to a container registry (e.g., Docker Hub or AWS ECR).
3. **Update Kubernetes Deployment**:

o   Update the Kubernetes deployment with the new image version and apply the changes using `kubectl`.

Here's an example of a **GitHub Actions workflow** to automate deployment to **Kubernetes**:

```yaml
name: Deploy to Kubernetes

on:
  push:
    branches:
      - main

jobs:
  deploy:
    runs-on: ubuntu-latest

    steps:
      - name: Checkout code
        uses: actions/checkout@v2

      - name: Build Docker image
        run: |
          docker build -t myapp:$GITHUB_SHA .

      - name: Push Docker image to Docker Hub
```

```
run: |
    docker        login        -u        ${{
secrets.DOCKER_USERNAME      }}      -p        ${{
secrets.DOCKER_PASSWORD }}
        docker push myapp:$GITHUB_SHA


- name: Deploy to Kubernetes
  run: |
      kubectl   set   image   deployment/myapp
myapp=myapp:$GITHUB_SHA
```

In this example:

- **Builds the Docker image** and tags it with the current commit SHA.
- **Pushes the image to Docker Hub**.
- **Updates the Kubernetes deployment** to use the new Docker image.

23.4 Summary

Concept	Description
Unit Testing in Go	Use Go's testing package to write unit tests and measure code performance.

Concept	Description
Integration Testing in Go	Test interactions between components, such as database and external service integration.
CI/CD Setup with GitHub Actions	Automate testing and deployment workflows using GitHub Actions.
Automating Deployments	Automate deployments to platforms like Heroku, Docker, and Kubernetes for faster releases.

Next Chapter: Monitoring and Debugging Go Applications

In the next chapter, we will:

- Set up **monitoring** for Go applications using tools like **Prometheus** and **Grafana**.
- Learn about **distributed tracing** with **Jaeger**.
- Explore **debugging techniques** for identifying and solving performance issues in Go applications.

CHAPTER 24

BUILDING SCALABLE REAL-TIME APPLICATIONS WITH WEBSOCKETS

Real-time applications are crucial in today's digital world, offering users live interaction and data updates. **WebSockets** provide a full-duplex communication channel over a single TCP connection, enabling real-time data exchange between the server and client. In this chapter, we will explore:

- **Introduction to WebSockets in Go**
- **Building a real-time chat application**
- **Handling real-time data streaming**

24.1 Introduction to WebSockets in Go

24.1.1 What is WebSocket?

WebSocket is a protocol that provides full-duplex communication channels over a single TCP connection. It is ideal for building real-time applications like chat applications, live notifications, and collaborative tools. Unlike traditional HTTP requests where the client initiates a request and the server responds, WebSocket allows bi-directional communication. The server can push updates to the client without waiting for a request.

24.1.2 WebSocket Flow

1. **Client sends a handshake request** to the server via HTTP to establish a WebSocket connection.
2. **Server accepts the connection** and upgrades the HTTP connection to a WebSocket connection.
3. **Client and server exchange messages** freely until one side closes the connection.

24.1.3 Advantages of WebSockets

- **Low Latency**: Since the connection is kept open, there's minimal delay in sending and receiving messages.
- **Reduced Overhead**: WebSockets have less overhead than HTTP, as they don't need to establish a new connection for every interaction.
- **Scalable**: WebSockets enable real-time communication across large numbers of clients with minimal resource usage.

24.1.4 WebSocket Libraries for Go

In Go, the most popular library for handling WebSockets is `gorilla/websocket`. It is simple, well-documented, and widely used in production applications.

sh

```
go get github.com/gorilla/websocket
```

24.2 Building a Real-Time Chat Application

In this section, we'll build a simple **real-time chat application** using WebSockets. The server will handle multiple clients, allowing them to send messages to each other in real time.

24.2.1 Setting Up the Project

Create a new Go project and initialize a Go module:

sh

```
mkdir go-chat-app
cd go-chat-app
go mod init go-chat-app
```

24.2.2 WebSocket Server in Go

We will create a simple WebSocket server that handles client connections and broadcasts messages to all connected clients.

```go
package main

import (
    "fmt"
    "log"
    "net/http"
    "github.com/gorilla/websocket"
)

var clients = make(map[*websocket.Conn]bool) // Connected clients
var broadcast = make(chan Message) // Broadcast channel

// Define a Message structure
type Message struct {
    Username string `json:"username"`
    Content  string `json:"content"`
}

// WebSocket handler
func handleConnections(w http.ResponseWriter, r *http.Request) {
```

```go
    ws, err := websocket.Upgrader{
        CheckOrigin: func(r *http.Request) bool
{ return true },
    }.Upgrade(w, r, nil)
    if err != nil {
        fmt.Println("Error              upgrading
connection:", err)
        return
    }
    defer ws.Close()

    clients[ws] = true

    for {
        var msg Message
        if err := ws.ReadJSON(&msg); err != nil
{
            fmt.Println("Error              reading
message:", err)
            delete(clients, ws)
            break
        }

        broadcast <- msg
    }
}

// Broadcast messages to all connected clients
func handleMessages() {
```

```go
    for {
        msg := <-broadcast
        for client := range clients {
            if err := client.WriteJSON(msg); err
!= nil {
                fmt.Println("Error         writing
message:", err)
                client.Close()
                delete(clients, client)
            }
        }
    }
}

func main() {
    // Set up WebSocket handler
    http.HandleFunc("/ws", handleConnections)

    // Start the message broadcaster
    go handleMessages()

    // Start the server
    log.Println("Server started on :8080")
    if err := http.ListenAndServe(":8080", nil);
err != nil {
        log.Fatal("Error starting server:", err)
    }
}
```

24.2.3 Explanation of Code

1. **handleConnections**:
   - Upgrades the incoming HTTP request to a WebSocket connection.
   - Adds the WebSocket connection to the `clients` map and listens for messages from the client.
2. **handleMessages**:
   - Reads messages from the `broadcast` channel and sends them to all connected clients.
3. **Broadcasting**:
   - When a message is received from one client, it is broadcast to all other connected clients using the WebSocket connection.

24.2.4 Running the Server

To start the server, run:

```sh

```

```
go run main.go
```

The server will listen on `http://localhost:8080`, and clients can connect to it using WebSocket.

24.2.5 Client-Side Code (HTML + JavaScript)

Create a simple client interface in HTML and JavaScript to connect to the WebSocket server.

html

```
<!DOCTYPE html>
<html lang="en">
<head>
    <meta charset="UTF-8">
    <title>Go Chat App</title>
</head>
<body>
    <h2>Real-Time Chat</h2>
    <input    id="username"    placeholder="Enter
username" />
    <textarea    id="message"    placeholder="Type
your message"></textarea>
    <button
onclick="sendMessage()">Send</button>
    <ul id="chat"></ul>

    <script>
        const       ws       =       new
WebSocket('ws://localhost:8080/ws');
        const        chat        =
document.getElementById('chat');
```

```
ws.onmessage = function(event) {
    const msg = JSON.parse(event.data);
    const              li              =
document.createElement('li');
    li.textContent = msg.username + ': '
+ msg.content;
    chat.appendChild(li);
};


function sendMessage() {
    const        username        =
document.getElementById('username').value;
    const        message         =
document.getElementById('message').value;
    ws.send(JSON.stringify({   username:
username, content: message }));
}
    </script>
</body>
</html>
```

24.2.6 Explanation of the Client-Side Code

- The client connects to the WebSocket server at `ws://localhost:8080/ws`.
- When the user sends a message, it is sent to the server through the WebSocket connection.
- The `onmessage` event handler listens for incoming messages from the server and updates the chat interface.

303

24.3 Handling Real-Time Data Streaming

WebSockets can also be used to handle **real-time data streaming** for applications like stock price updates, live sports scores, or any real-time notifications.

24.3.1 Streaming Data with WebSockets

Imagine you're building an application to stream real-time stock prices. The server will push updates to connected clients whenever there's a change in stock prices.

Example: Stock Price Streaming Server

```go
package main

import (
    "fmt"
    "log"
    "time"
    "github.com/gorilla/websocket"
)

var clients = make(map[*websocket.Conn]bool)
var broadcast = make(chan Message)
```

```go
type Message struct {
    Symbol string `json:"symbol"`
    Price  float64 `json:"price"`
}


func handleConnections(w http.ResponseWriter, r
*http.Request) {
    ws, err := websocket.Upgrader{
        CheckOrigin: func(r *http.Request) bool
{ return true },
    }.Upgrade(w, r, nil)
    if err != nil {
        fmt.Println("Error              upgrading
connection:", err)
        return
    }
    defer ws.Close()

    clients[ws] = true

    // Send stock price updates every 5 seconds
    ticker := time.NewTicker(5 * time.Second)
    defer ticker.Stop()

    for {
        select {
        case <-ticker.C:
            price := Message{Symbol:   "AAPL",
Price: 145.32}  // Example stock price
```

```go
            broadcast <- price
        }
    }
}


func handleMessages() {
    for {
        msg := <-broadcast
        for client := range clients {
            if err := client.WriteJSON(msg); err
!= nil {
                fmt.Println("Error        writing
message:", err)
                client.Close()
                delete(clients, client)
            }
        }
    }
}


func main() {
    http.HandleFunc("/ws", handleConnections)
    go handleMessages()

    log.Println("Server started on :8080")
    if err := http.ListenAndServe(":8080", nil);
err != nil {
        log.Fatal("Error starting server:", err)
    }
```

}

Explanation:

- The **ticker** sends stock price updates to the `broadcast` channel every 5 seconds.
- Each client receives updates about the stock price in real time.

24.3.2 Scaling for Real-Time Data

When handling large numbers of concurrent WebSocket connections, it's crucial to scale the WebSocket server. To handle **scalable real-time data streaming**, you can:

- Use **Load Balancing** to distribute WebSocket connections across multiple server instances.
- Use **message brokers** like **Kafka** or **Redis Pub/Sub** to handle the distribution of real-time events.

24.4 Summary

Concept	Description
WebSockets in Go	WebSockets allow real-time, full-duplex communication between clients and

Concept	Description
	servers, ideal for chat applications and live updates.
Real-Time Chat Application	Example of building a WebSocket-based chat app, handling multiple clients and broadcasting messages in real time.
Data Streaming with WebSockets	Use WebSockets to stream real-time data such as stock prices or notifications to clients.
Scalability Considerations	For high concurrency and data streaming, use load balancing, message brokers, and scalable architecture patterns.

Next Chapter: Advanced Topics in Web Development with Go

In the next chapter, we will:

- Explore **WebSocket scaling strategies**.
- Dive into **real-time data processing** techniques for large-scale applications.

- Learn how to build **distributed systems** with Go for real-time applications.

CHAPTER 25

THE FUTURE OF GO AND FINAL THOUGHTS

Go has been a highly popular language for systems programming, cloud-native applications, and microservices architectures. As Go continues to evolve, new features and improvements are on the horizon. In this final chapter, we will explore:

- **Upcoming Go features and improvements**
- **How Go fits into modern software development**
- **Best resources to keep learning Go**

25.1 Upcoming Go Features and Improvements

The Go programming language is known for its simplicity, speed, and robust concurrency model. The Go team has made significant strides in improving these features over the years. As we look to the future, here are some of the upcoming features and improvements in Go.

25.1.1 Go 1.18+ and the Introduction of Generics

One of the most anticipated features in Go's development is the introduction of **Generics** (in Go 1.18). Generics allow developers to write more flexible and reusable code, enabling functions, data structures, and algorithms to operate on different data types without sacrificing type safety. The implementation of Generics in Go will make it easier to create libraries that work with any data type without repeating code.

- **Why Generics Matter**: They provide better code reusability and flexibility, and are particularly useful for collections, algorithms, and reusable components.

Key Highlights of Generics in Go:

- **Type Parameters**: Functions and types can now be parameterized by types.
- **Type Constraints**: Generics in Go are constrained, meaning you can limit what types can be used with a given function or type.
- **Improved Libraries**: Libraries that require generics (like `container/list`, `map`, etc.) can become more efficient, easier to maintain, and less verbose.

25.1.2 Performance Improvements

Go's performance is one of its biggest strengths, and the Go team continues to focus on making the language faster while maintaining its simplicity and ease of use.

- **Garbage Collection (GC) Improvements**: The Go team is working to further optimize the garbage collector for **low-latency applications** and **multi-core processors**.
- **Compilation Speed**: The Go team continually focuses on improving the speed of compilation without compromising the performance of the code it generates.
- **Memory Efficiency**: Efforts are being made to reduce memory footprint and improve the performance of Go programs, particularly in cloud-native and embedded systems.

25.1.3 Enhancements in Tooling and Debugging

Go is already known for having great tooling, and future improvements will focus on making the debugging experience even better. The Go team is working to provide:

- **Better Profiling Tools**: Enhancing existing profiling tools like **pprof** for better insight into performance bottlenecks.
- **Improved Debugging**: Debugging tools for Go are becoming more feature-rich, with better integration into

IDEs and enhanced debugging support for concurrent programs.

25.2 How Go Fits Into Modern Software Development

25.2.1 Cloud-Native and Microservices

Go has become a **top choice** for building **cloud-native applications** and **microservices** due to its simplicity, speed, and robust support for concurrency. In an era where applications must scale, Go shines in the following areas:

- **Concurrency**: Go's goroutines and channels make it ideal for building highly concurrent applications, especially when handling a large number of microservices.
- **Performance**: Go is compiled to native machine code, meaning it offers great performance compared to interpreted languages like Python or Ruby.
- **Ecosystem**: Go's ecosystem includes powerful libraries and frameworks for building scalable cloud-native applications, such as **Kubernetes**, **Docker**, and **Prometheus**.

25.2.2 Integration with Modern Architectures

Go plays a key role in building distributed systems, data pipelines, and high-performance backends. Its ability to interact seamlessly with other languages and frameworks makes it a great choice for modern software development.

- **API Services**: Go excels at building high-performance RESTful and gRPC APIs.
- **Real-time Systems**: With WebSockets, Go is used to build real-time applications like chat systems, notification services, and live data dashboards.
- **Cloud Infrastructure**: Many **cloud platforms** (like AWS Lambda, Google Cloud Functions) and **service orchestration tools** (like Kubernetes) have Go at their core.

25.2.3 Go in the IoT and Embedded Systems Space

Due to its small binary size and efficient memory management, Go is increasingly being used in **IoT** (Internet of Things) and **embedded systems**. Its cross-platform support and simplicity make it a great choice for developers building software that runs on constrained devices, such as sensors, gateways, and other embedded devices.

25.3 Best Resources to Keep Learning Go

The Go language continues to evolve, and it's important to keep learning and stay up-to-date with the latest developments. Here are some of the best resources for continuing your Go journey.

25.3.1 Official Go Documentation and Resources

- **Go Documentation**: The official Go documentation is a comprehensive guide to learning Go. It covers everything from basic syntax to advanced topics like concurrency and networking.
  - o URL: https://golang.org/doc/
- **Go Wiki**: The Go Wiki on GitHub contains additional resources and best practices for Go developers.
  - o URL: https://github.com/golang/go/wiki
- **Go Blog**: The official Go blog provides insights into language updates, real-world use cases, and performance tips.
  - o URL: https://blog.golang.org/

25.3.2 Books for Learning Go

- **"Go Programming Language" by Alan A. A. Donovan and Brian W. Kernighan**: This book is one of the most recommended for Go developers. It's written by the creators of the language and provides a deep dive into Go programming.

- **"Go in Action" by William Kennedy**: This book covers Go fundamentals and dives into real-world applications of Go, including web development and concurrency.

- **"Learning Go" by Jon Bodner**: A beginner-friendly book that helps you get up and running with Go quickly, including best practices and real-world projects.

25.3.3 Online Tutorials and Courses

- **Go by Example**: A hands-on tutorial website that provides a collection of examples for various Go concepts.
  - o URL: https://gobyexample.com/

- **Exercism.io**: A platform that offers Go exercises with mentorship. It's a great way to learn by doing and getting feedback from experienced Go developers.
  - o URL: https://exercism.io/tracks/go

- **Udemy**: Several great courses are available for learning Go on Udemy, including **"Go: The Complete Developer's Guide"** by Stephen Grider.
  - o URL: https://www.udemy.com/
- **Pluralsight**: Offers courses such as **"Go Fundamentals"** and **"Go Web Development"** that cover the essentials as well as advanced topics.
  - o URL: https://www.pluralsight.com/

25.3.4 Go Community and Forums

- **Go Forum**: An active community of Go developers where you can ask questions, share insights, and discuss Go topics.
  - o URL: https://forum.golang.org/
- **Go Subreddit**: The Go subreddit is a great place to stay up-to-date on Go news, discuss best practices, and share resources.
  - o URL: https://www.reddit.com/r/golang/
- **Stack Overflow**: A great platform for getting answers to your Go-specific questions from experienced developers.
  - o URL: https://stackoverflow.com/questions/tagged/go

25.4 Final Thoughts

Go has proven to be an excellent language for building efficient, scalable, and concurrent applications. With its simplicity, strong ecosystem, and growing adoption in various domains such as microservices, cloud computing, and embedded systems, Go is poised to remain a key player in the software development world.

As Go continues to evolve with features like **Generics**, **performance optimizations**, and **better concurrency models**, it is essential to keep learning and experimenting with new tools and patterns in Go.

Whether you are building high-performance web servers, real-time applications, or cloud-native solutions, Go provides a solid foundation to create reliable and efficient software.

Next Steps

- **Explore advanced Go topics** such as Go's internals, compiler optimizations, and deep dive into Go's concurrency patterns.

- **Start contributing** to open-source Go projects to improve your skills and give back to the community.
- Stay updated with the latest **Go releases** and **community discussions** to keep up with language improvements and new tools.

Thank you for following along in this journey to mastering Go!

www.ingramcontent.com/pod-product-compliance
Lightning Source LLC
LaVergne TN
LVHW051432050326
832903LV00030BD/3035

* 9 7 9 8 3 1 3 5 5 8 8 5 1 *